Fine... I'll Talk With You

FINE... I'LL TALK WITH YOU

interviews with Pulitzer, Oscar, and Tony winning
playwrights and screenwriters

by Kevin Hylton

2019

to the playwrights who gave their time to this project,

to my mom, baba, karel, george, mike, and jared for all the support,

jenn who reads everything I write and makes it better,

libby and sara - if you imagine it, you can make it happen

Contents:

Contents:

"If one advances confidently in the direction of his dreams, and endeavors to live the life which he has imagined, he will meet with a success unexpected in common hours."

-Henry David Thoreau, <u>Walden</u>

Introduction

Reproduced Email from Pulitzer Prize Winning Playwright:

From: Unnamed Pulitzer Prize Winning Playwright

To: Kevin Hylton

Re: Interview Request- For Book of Interviews

Date: May 1, 2007

Fine... I'll talk with you.

So clearly he was excited to meet with me. Ha. I wasn't surprised. When I approached this Unnamed Pulitzer Prize Winner for an interview, my credentials included a few articles for <u>Playbill</u> magazine, a piece in a pop culture magazine that went under in five issues, and a steady, unpaid gig as the theater columnist for a website entitled "<u>Moviepoopshoot.com</u>." In retrospect, it's rather shocking that he replied to my request at all. Come to think of it, what agent in his or her right mind even passed my info on to him?

Sitting here, now ten years after I first published this collection, I am still dumbfounded that these writers all agreed to meet with me. But I guess that's the point of this whole book. Persistence pays off.

Back in the early 2000's I started submitting some of my own plays and screenplays to agents and theaters. I received many rejection letters and read numerous "how to get produced" books from people who didn't have much success themselves. After a couple of years building up the stack of "no thank you's," I realized that my current path was getting me nowhere. A couple of thoughts crossed my mind. Should I go back to school for a degree in screenwriting or playwriting? If so, where should I go? Is there a better route? I figured I should ask someone who had some success in writing for film and theater how they did it. Maybe they could point me in the right direction.

But, wait. Why on earth would these writers meet with me? They've won Oscars, Pulitzer Prizes, and Tony Awards. I regularly get rejection letters written to the wrong person. No one knows who I am. How could I create a platform? Hmm... maybe I could beg my friend to let me write another article for Playbill. Done. Great. But two articles doesn't give me much street cred. Now what? I know... I need a regular column so I can get set up with interviews, tickets to shows, and scathing blog comments about my columns. Let's see, maybe I should email the editor of filmmaker Kevin Smith's webosite Moviepoopshoot.com. "Hey Editor. You don't have a theater columnist. I could be such a person. I want to interview all of the film industry people who are currently working on Broadway. Sure, I've written columns before. I just wrote an article for Playbill. No money to pay me? No problem. Let's call it *'From Screen to Stage.'*" Done.

"Hi Mr. Publicity Agent. I write for Moviepoopshoot.com. We get millions of viewer hits annually. I want to interview David Mamet about his new play. Oh, sure I understand he won't speak with me. Do you have any other Hollywood folks working in theater productions on or Off-Broadway who would like some press? Yes, it is really called 'Moviepoopshoot.com'. "

Cut to several years later. I had built an audience of at least three people. I received the email that started this introduction chapter on a cold Sunday morning, started lining up other interviewees, got an agent, circulated proposals through big publishers, was rejected by publishers for not having a significant enough platform, got dropped by said agent, got picked up by one of the interviewees' agents, recirculated my book proposal, and got dropped by new agent while she was in the hospital. And now I am sitting here writing this updated introduction ten years later. Today I can get people to read my screenplays and have had my writing produced by Disney. I'm currently developing film and television projects and things have changed in the world for myself and humanity since I started doing the interviews for this book, some fifteen years ago.

At the end of the day, you'll this book will show you that everyone's path to success in the entertainment industry is different. I don't attempt to offer any analysis of the writers' experiences in this book. I will tell you that when you compare the stories of these professionals, there are many common threads to their paths which may prove valuable to readers looking for career advice. So for those of you looking for a "how to break into the industry book," this is a good start. For those of you interested in autobiographies, the book you are reading details how some of our finest screenwriters and playwrights got their starts in the entertainment industry. And for those of you history enthusiasts, the following interviews will provide you with information on how Off-Broadway, Broadway, and the Film Industry has evolved over the last eighty years.

Whatever your reason for opening this book, I hope you enjoy getting to know these authors as much as I have. I am grateful not only for the time they spent with me discussing their paths but everything they have contributed to the industries.

Fine... I'll Talk With You

HORTON FOOTE

Horton Foote was born in Wharton, Texas in 1916. He won Oscars for Best Screenplay for his films <u>To Kill A Mockingbird</u> (1962) and <u>Tender Mercies</u> (1984), as well as a Pulitzer Prize for his play <u>The Young Man From Atlanta</u> (1995). He had numerous other screenplays, teleplays, and stage plays produced in New York before his death on March 4, 2009. The most comprehensive biographical piece on the playwright was written by Foote himself and is titled, <u>Genesis Of An American Playwright</u> (Baylor University Press, 2004). Through a series of essays and lectures composed by Horton, the playwright examines his life, background, and a variety of issues pertinent to the theater and film worlds. The following interview focuses on the years between 1938 and 1955 which were not discussed in detail in his autobiography. It was during those years that Horton saw his writing career truly take flight.

Chapter One

Afternoon, New York City

FOOTE: I was trained as an actor by the Russians.
When I was starting out there was no official Off-
Broadway. There were a group of us trying to put
together a company. So we rented a little garage on 69th
Street and we called ourselves "The American Actors
Company." And we went away for the summer of 1938
and worked on exercises and improvisations that would
become a play. The play was Edith Hamilton's
translation of The Trojan Women.

We raised money and put it on a small stage in New York
City. Sadly, it was not a critical success. But in the
process we met a woman named Mary Hunter, who later
became Mary Hunter Wolfe. She was the niece of the
novelist Mary Austin. She lived in Chicago and knew
other novelists and we were fortunate to be surrounded
by some very interesting actors. Eventually, while I was
doing improvisational acting for the theater, Agnes
DeMille, who was planning a future production for the
group with Mary, suggested that I write a play for the
group [the play, Wharton Dance].

To make a long story short, critics came to see it and liked it and the play was done on a stage on 16th Street. And that somewhat started me off as a playwright. So in a sense I was a promising playwright, but I hadn't really done much. I had to learn a lot of lessons. I became friendly with Tennessee Williams through the American Actors Company. But he knew me as an actor, because when I met him I was still an actor.

I would ask him a lot of questions. And he was very kind to me. And then he let me [act in] a play of his then called The Gentlemen Caller [which later became The Glass Menagerie]. I worked with him very closely, which was outstanding. While in New York with the American Actors Company I became friendly with dancers, choreographers, and others who knew about a performance space in Washington, DC. And I decided that I wanted to get out of New York and make my own space away from the crowd. By that time I had become very heavily influenced by dance. I had been commissioned to do a play, which I co-directed with a choreographer and that was a great influence.

I very much wanted to experiment in theater at that point in my life. So my wife and I went down to DC, in 1945, and we all started this little company. We had a school that helped finance it [the King-Smith School]. I was there for five years and was free to do anything I wanted theatrically. It was a great learning experience. I was fortunate because I could experiment a lot. I had freedom. I did very experimental stuff at that time and I guess I got it out of my system.

Soon thereafter I went back to more realistic theater and I wrote a play that found its way to New York. That didn't

go anywhere, but it got the ball rolling and led me back to
New York City.

HYLTON: Can you tell me a little more about your
experimental work?

FOOTE: I did a commission for the Neighborhood
Playhouse and at the end of the year they produced a
piece for me. So they commissioned me to write a play
with a score written by Lori Hart and directed and
choreographed by Valerie Dennis. That was pretty heady
company for a young playwright in his early twenties. If
they asked me to do the same thing now I'd fall over
dead, I'd be so nervous. But at that time I was shockingly
able. So, I did that and I did a ballet for the same
director. She was very interested in re-defining theater.
The work was called Daisy Lee. Then I befriended
Jerome Robbins.

After I went back to New York [Jerome] called me and
asked me if I would do something for Nora Kaye to
dance and act in for a review she was doing with Bette
Davis called Two's Company. And I did that and it was
the last I ever did in dance until a few years ago when
Twyla Thorpe called me and asked if I would work on a
piece with her. We came up with a piece, but it was going
to cost a million dollars to do it and we couldn't afford it.
So it didn't work out.

HYLTON: I'm interested in the time you spent in
Washington, DC working in the theater and starting a
school.

FOOTE: It was called the King-Smith school. It was a
very fancy girls school. And then eventually boys started

22

to go to the school. When I came along, they switched it to an arts school with painting and dancing and classes in literature and theater. It was on New Hampshire Avenue. I lived in an apartment about five houses down from the school. They also had rooms in their main building that they rented to ladies, young and old. And they gave night courses. Valerie [Foote] was the dance teacher and a man named Greg Green was in charge of the music side while I was there. I'm still all for experimental theater and although I don't work that way anymore, I still like to go and see some.

HYLTON: Did you try to keep your hands in New York while you were living in D.C.?

FOOTE: No, I didn't. I had an agent but the next phase, when I look back, was something not planned at all. It was the early television days back then. And that time was very kind to me. I have always loved the one act form. And back in those days nobody ever wanted one act plays. But when television came along there was a great need for certain kinds of stories. And I did about ten one act plays that were all published to this day. I wrote them when I was back in New York.

HYLTON: Did you continue with your old New York theater group when you returned to Manhattan from DC?

FOOTE: No, unfortunately it dissolved. But we had wonderful people back then. So, I left Washington and came back to New York because I had a three-act play called The Chase, which was being produced in New York. At that time television was just looking around for writers. So I, along with Gore Vidal and a couple of others, were gathered together and given free rein to write for the shows. That was all live television. It was very much like theater at the time. They did not have the ability at that point to tape, edit, and rebroadcast like they do now.

HYLTON: I understand you direct your own plays from time to time. How do you decide which projects you will direct and which of your pieces you will pass on to other directors?

FOOTE: I do make choices. But it's that crazy word "instinct." I wouldn't know how to make it logical. There were just certain things of my own that I really would not want to do while there were other things which I am very happy directing. I just think that if you are happy doing it and your work does not suffer by it, then you should do it. I certainly think there is value to doing this kind of work. If nothing more, it makes you a little more humble to the job and value of a director.

HYLTON: What kind of role do you play in the theater during the rehearsals and pre-production stage when you're not directing?

FOOTE: I am enormously sympathetic to the problems that present themselves to be solved. And I am more than happy to try and help with anything. But I never take the position of the adversary because I think that isn't helpful to anybody. Usually, I am part of the casting apparatus, so I help with that. I just find the whole event very exciting, meeting the actors, and seeing them read. So I like to be involved on that end. I just don't think that there is any one way to do anything in that respect. I think if it's a great actor, or any actor for that matter, the person can bring something extra to your part. And it may be very different from what someone else brings to the part. There's more than one way to skin a cat I suppose.

HYLTON: Do you attempt to rewrite?

FOOTE: I don't attempt to rewrite ever. But if I'm in the room and something is not working, I try and fix it.

HYLTON: Do you have the play all worked out prior to a reading?

FOOTE: Yes, sure but I sometimes do rework based on what the actors come up with. Particularly if it's someone who I really respect, because this is a collaborative medium. And I think you're fooling yourself if you think any one person can do everything. So I try to be as open as possible because it is interesting to get all the help that you can.

HYLTON: Is it difficult for you to turn your work over to another director after you've completed the play?

FOOTE: Well, it's not really turning it over. I think the first thing a playwright and director need to learn about is how to have a good collaboration. I want the best director I can have. I don't want a director I can push around. But I also want a director who will allow collaboration by the actors and myself as well.

HYLTON: Can you tell me a bit about your experiences teaching playwriting?

FOOTE: I guess that playwriting, well, I don't know. When I came back to New York from Washington there was a thing called the American Theater Wing. So I was asked by the director to teach the playwriting course there. And I did that for some time. That was a good experience for me and I hope for the students as well. But many of them had been bouncing from playwriting class to playwriting class, having every playwriting teacher in creation teach them essentially the same things. They came to me and asked me for advice and I don't know if it was good or not. Many of them were going from class to class with the same play trying to figure out how to make it, rather than actually writing. I so love writing so it's very hard for me to understand the difficulties that other people have with writing.

HYLTON: In your book you spoke about how you wish you could have started as a writer in today's theater world, rather than when you began. How has the theater world changed since you started?

FOOTE: It's just so different. There were no Off-Broadway venues then and you just didn't have the same type of resources available then. But now it's so commercial. Back then regional theater did not exist in the same way either. And it does make some sense with the focus on the commercial side of the work. Because when they take plays out of town, people are only willing to see a play written by a playwright of note and a playwright of note that they are familiar with.

Once your play has shown they all run down to you and tell you exactly what was wrong with it. I don't know. I think the only two playwrights whose work really succeeds on the regional stages are Tennessee [Williams] and Arthur [Miller]. I mean do you ever hear about anyone doing Robert Sherwood? I could go down a list of them. But there are so many skillfully written plays that are more interesting than the plays that make their way to Broadway. But that's neither here nor there.

HYLTON: Do you think audiences and producers are open to a different type of play today?

FOOTE: Well, I think that there is much more competition now, but there are more venues now also. And oh my god, the cost now of putting on a show is just so much more expensive and, well, that changes everything. It's now a really difficult profession. Someone once said something very apropos, "You can make a killing in theater, but you can't make a living out of it."

WENDY WASSERSTEIN

Wendy Wasserstein was born in Brooklyn, New York in 1950. After attending a Yeshiva in Brooklyn, NY and then transferring to an all-girls high school, Wendy made her way to Mount Holyoke College. Later, she became one of the first women to attend Yale's Playwriting MFA program. In 1989 Wendy's The Heidi Chronicles won the Pulitzer Prize for Drama. She responded by spending the next two decades writing an extensive collection of provocative plays, screenplays, and novels. I met Wendy Wasserstein in the winter of 2005 on the Upper West Side of Manhattan, just a couple of months before she passed away. On February 6, 2006 Charlie Rose dedicated an hour-long memorial episode to Wendy's honor. He described her as the type of person who "when they are gone, you profoundly feel something missing, more than you might ever have expected."

Chapter Two

Morning, New York City

HYLTON: I want to start by asking you about a friend of yours. Tell me about Chris Durang.

WASSERSTEIN: Chris and I met at Yale Drama School. He was two years ahead of me. When I got there in 1973, which was my first year, it was his last year. But then he stayed the following year in New Haven because he won a fellowship. So we were really in New Haven for two years together.

HYLTON: That's a long time to be in New Haven.

WASSERSTEIN: Christopher and I used to say we couldn't have invented a New Haven. One summer Christopher and I got crazy jobs together. We got jobs working at an employment agency and we got these jobs doing coding for the School of Public Health at Yale. You know, when you look at surveys and you code them. We did them for medical graduates. And then he and I would take a ride out to Tweed Airport (New Haven Airport) to drink milkshakes. I have really fond memories of those summers in New Haven with Chris.

HYLTON: I read that your mother was an influence in you starting to write.

WASSERSTEIN: I think my mother is the most theatrical person I know. I've for a long time wanted to write a play about my mother, but I have not yet. She's a character in Isn't It Romantic. But I have not given her a full play yet. But she's amazing. She was a professional dancer and she still dances. Well, let me put it this way… I'm in my fifties and I am the youngest of her children. So, my mother still dances at the Broadway Dance Center. And I've had auditions with multiple people who came in and said, "Oh, I've danced with your mother. And she's a hoot." She enjoys her own theatricality and sexuality. She's this weird combination of "Get married! Get married!" and this real independence and deep eccentricity. I mean deep eccentricity. This is not forced. I mean my mother was an immigrant. I just find her fascinating.

When Chris Durang met my mother, well, let me go back a step. When we were in drama school Chris and I used to go out to dinner together. That's how we became friends. We would tell each other stories about our families. So, I was brought up going to a pretty conservative Jewish high school in New York. I went to Flatbush Yeshiva. Then I went to another high school in New York.

Everything I learned [about art] was from Chris Durang, as far as I can make out. So Chris was curious to meet my family and one time [my mom] came up to see me. And honest to god, I don't know why she did this, but one time when she came up to see me she was dressed as Patty Hearst. She was wearing a beret. She was carrying a plastic toy gun. She looked just like Patty Hearst. She walked in and said to Chris, "Who am I?" And I was really pleased at that moment because I thought to myself, "She has just verified the picture I painted of her for Chris." So, yes, my mother was a great influence with her theatrical personality.

My mother sent me to dancing school. She sent me to the June Taylor dancing school on Saturdays. But she made me lie to the Rabbi and say that I went to temple on Saturday. I used to cry to her and ask, "Why do I have to lie to the principal of the school about this?" Who would make their child do that? I'm not that interesting. I'm not. I'm just a good girl. I just couldn't do that but she had me lie to the Rabbi. And so he'd ask me on Monday, "Did you go to shul?" And I'd say, "Yes." But meanwhile I had been dancing away on Saturday. I think, given my dancing abilities, I would have been better off going to shul.

My mother is dramatic, eccentric, and deeply funny. She's just really, really funny, but with an edge. She is much funnier than I am.

HYLTON: I heard your grandfather was a writer as well.

WASSERSTEIN: Yes, he wrote plays. Unfortunately, my grandmother lost them. My grandparents were from Poland. They came here and I think my grandfather was an actor in Pittsburgh for a while. Somehow he ended up as the principal of a Hebrew School in New Jersey. But he knew the people in the Yiddish theater. He used to take my mother to the theater. He knew all of the people involved. While I was in college I met a guy who was from a Yiddish Tradition in Winnipeg and somehow his father knew of my grandfather's work. And there was someone who my mother talks about who was a translator who went, well, I should qualify this because my mother's mind is, well… When I won the Pulitzer my mother said to friends that I had won the Nobel Prize. So she claims that someone from Columbia had translated my grandfather's plays. Sadly, we do not have any of them.

HYLTON: When was it that you started writing plays?

WASSERSTEIN: I started writing plays when I was in high school. At this point I was at Calhoon, which was an all girls high school, and there was something they had every year called the Mother/Daughter fashion show. I figured out if I wrote a show I wouldn't have to dance. So I wrote a show. But in elementary school I was in a lot of plays. And it's funny, because I am currently looking at elementary schools for my daughter and it shows you how that early education really affects your mind.

Oddly enough, Patty Condon and I went to the same elementary school. She went the first year it opened. It was called the Clifton Culture School. It was on Prospect Park West. And there literally was a woman in the back of the school room with a drum beating on it. So she would beat on the drum and, as she did, we would say aloud the names of poets. I love Patty. She and I are still good friends. And she says that for the rest of her life she's been very creative. I think that if you exercise one side of your brain it develops.

So when I was in high school I wrote some plays. When I was in college I had a really good playwriting professor.

That's really what happened to me. I was at Mount Holyoke and had a great teacher.

HYLTON: Suzan-Lori Parks was at Holyoke as well wasn't she?

WASSERSTEIN: Yes. Well you know what's interesting about Holyoke? Holyoke is a very traditional woman's college. It is not an arts school. It is not a Sarah Lawrence. Yet both myself and Suzan-Lori Parks, these two contemporary women who won the Pulitzer, came from that school and both came from very different backgrounds. So I think it's interesting to ask, "Why is that true?" And then you get back to, "So is it about art or is it about confidence in your own voice?" And with women, at that period, maybe it had to do more with confidence in your own voice and confidence in women. And I think that's a very interesting topic to investigate.

HYLTON: Do you think that's different today?

WASSERSTEIN: I don't know. I mean, I don't know that much about contemporary women's education. But I found the parallel between myself and Suzan-Lori Parks very interesting. As I say, Holyoke was by no means an arts school. And until 1971 Holyoke had the highest percentage of women who became doctors. And even compared to Smith or Vassar or the other women's colleges… well, it's just interesting.

I was taking a class to become a Congressional Intern. And I was falling asleep reading the Congressional Digest. I didn't do very well in college. I didn't get great grades or anything. And it probably was too traditional for me, but also this was the late sixties. So at a groovy time, theater was decidedly un-groovy. But it was a time of change, clearly. But anyway, a friend of mine said why don't you take this class at Smith and then afterwards we can go shopping. And I took this class and I was just happy. The professor was a guy named Len Berkman who still teaches there. And he's a good playwright and a wonderful teacher.

I don't know that it's the best writing that I do. But what I liked about writing was it could be funny or it could be distant or ingratiating. It can be a lot of things. That's why I often try to write people who are humorous, because it's complicated. It's not blah, blah, blah, blah. It's "Why is the character behaving the way they are behaving in these circumstances, which may be very far from funny?" What I didn't know was that by taking this college playwriting course it made it legitimate.

I thought when I went to college you did it to go to law school. I didn't even have a sense that college was about getting an education to do something you like. I didn't even get a sense that you typically would like what you did for a living. But this playwriting course gave me that feeling. I put on plays at the Scarsdale Community Playhouse. And I thought to myself, I can really do this. So I think that made it legitimate.

I never saw myself as an artistic person. What's interesting is as I went on in life and met real artists like Chris Durang and William Finn or Terrance McNally, I thought "I'm not those people either." I think that back then I thought to be artistic I had to be one of them. And I'm not. And I've pretty much been writing plays since that class in 1969. Then I came to New York and I also went to City College and I took some playwriting courses from Joseph Heller.

HYLTON: So how did you approach getting your work produced when you moved to New York?

WASSERSTEIN: This is how I got my first play done. My mother was walking down the street and [she] ran into this woman named Louise Roberts. [Louise] used to be the receptionist at the June Taylor School of Dance, where I used to go. And Louise ran into my mom and asked, "How's Wendy?" My mom started hyperventilating. And Louise said "I work at a new dancing school and across the hall there's a new theater called Playwrights Horizons." Louise gave my play to Bob Vaughn and that's literally how the play got done. I had some good luck. And this was all at Playwrights Horizons before it moved to 42nd Street when it was at the Y on 52nd Street.

HYLTON: And then you went to Yale?

WASSERSTEIN: Yes, and then I went up to Yale Drama School for several years. And it was difficult. It was a difficult time. I don't think I was their favorite. I'm too ostensibly cheerful. But, I loved Howard Stein. He was wonderful and if you talk to other people from Yale, at that time, they will echo this. When you speak with Chris [Durang] ask him about Howard. I think for me, as a playwright, that's what solidified it all. That's where I wrote, Uncommon Women. I became very interested with women on stage. I think because I had gone to women's high school and college I wanted to write something where there was this huge change.

Chris and I used to go to movies a lot at the Yale Film Society. And we'd see these films like The Stage Door. Actually, women wrote a lot of them. And I was very interested in them because these were witty women and there was nothing in the literature we were reading about that. And I wanted to see an all women's curtain call at the end of the play. I am really glad I went [to Yale].

We had our plays read and did a lot of reading. I was very unhappy at the time. I mean there you are, from twenty-three to twenty-six, and you have no idea what is going to happen to you. And your other friends are in law school or med school and they are fine and adjusted. When you're a playwright, what you don't understand at twenty-six is you don't know what's going to happen to you for the rest of your life. So that was very difficult for me. It was very hard being there and not getting that.

[At Yale] we'd read scenes with the other playwrights and that was the same as class essentially. The program was started at Harvard and then came down to Yale. We felt like they didn't perform enough of our plays back then. We went in to see one of the professors and said, "You must do more of our plays." I think what was really valuable was the community of people there who I met. It was the first time I was with people who were like me. They have remained very important people in my life. Christopher, Tom Lynch... all of them are really important people to me.

I came back to New York [after graduating] and I had no idea what to do at that point. So a woman we knew at Yale had a sister named Nancy who was an administrator at the Eugene O'Neill Foundation. She helped me get a job as a messenger for the O'Neill Foundation. So when

I got out of Yale I literally delivered the scripts to the theaters. I was sent out to get coffee as well. I'm highly in favor of people who come out of drama school getting involved in something in the theater, in any capacity. If for no other reason it gives you a sounding board. I was running all over the place on the subway and bringing scripts to people and making contacts. I learned the intricacies of the process of production. Eventually I submitted Uncommon Women to the O'Neill.

I enjoyed the work. It was kooky. But I enjoyed the job and I met all sorts of people. I met tons of very interesting playwrights I would not have known. The O'Neill is a wonderful place. I was literally the gopher when Uncommon Women got done there. So I spent that summer at the O'Neill. That summer there were many good plays and there were some great directors working there. And Uncommon Women was done that summer. I remember that it used to be that all of the theater people would come up to see the plays at the O'Neill.

HYLTON: It's a very difficult festival to get into.

WASSERSTEIN: It's very difficult.

HYLTON: So how did the reading of Uncommon Women at the O'Neill lead to future work then?

WASSERSTEIN: Well, I went back to Playwrights Horizons and we re-did Isn't It Romantic. I chose to take Uncommon Women to the Phoenix Theater. And it was directed by Steve Rodman who directed it at the O'Neill. And Swoosie Kurtz, who was in it at the O'Neill, acted in it in New York. She won an Obie

Award for her performance. I mean we were twenty-seven years old then. The Phoenix production got wonderful notices and it ran for two and a half weeks. That was a little before things started to move on their own.

HYLTON: So you really didn't have to self-produce work then on your own?

WASSERSTEIN: I did the year I was "Miss Messenger." I sent plays all over the place. I got Uncommon Women rejected with postage due from The Mark Taper Forum. They wrote a silly note back saying something like, "Clearly you don't care about women." But I sent out plays all the time on my own back then. And they all got rejected. So I started to take Physics at Marymount College, because I thought I had no gift.

HYLTON: Physics?

WASSERSTEIN: Yeah, I got so many rejections I thought maybe I should become a Psychiatrist. I figured, "I'm a smart person. I can make myself do this." And, in fact, the stage they used for Uncommon Women in New York was at Marymount College. So I was taking classes at the same location where the play was being produced.

HYLTON: Well, I guess you had a backup plan.

WASSERSTEIN: Yeah, I had a backup plan.

HYLTON: Tell me a little bit about Playwrights Horizons and your experiences there.

WASSERSTEIN: Playwrights Horizons was started by
Bob Moss in a tiny Y on 52nd Street. And then the whole
42nd Street rebirth happened. Nobody acknowledged that
Moss was behind that rebirth, but he was. You know
they'll do some PBS or Channel 13 thing about Broadway
and say "And here's Michael Eisner who had the
foresight to…" But like any other change, it happens
first because some small artist starts it and then a big
corporation moves in. While I was at Yale I sent plays
out to theaters in New York. But the first play that I had
read was done at Playwrights and it was called Montpelier
Pizzazz. And thankfully you will never find a copy of this
play. But Playwrights Horizons remembered me.

When Bob Moss moved his theater to 42nd Street it was
still a Burlesque house. They did my play in a theater
festival and the first reading of Uncommon Women in
New York was upstairs in Playwrights Horizons. I read it
there before it was ever sent out anywhere. It was in the
same building as the Sex Institute of Technology. I have
a funny story about when my Dad came to see a reading
of my play. At intermission the guy collecting donations
for the theater came out with a paper bag and he asked
for money. So my dad was so upset about the situation
there on 42nd Street that he gave the guy fifty dollars to
help out. It was literally a burlesque house.

In 1980 Walter Mondale came to christen the new 42nd
Street theater. And they had me write a short play called
Writer's Block. It starred Mimi Kennedy and we did it on
the street. And it had Bob Moss singing "Forty upah,
upah, Second." And Mondale came with a bottle of
champagne and christened the block. It was a very
different time.

HYLTON: Do you still stay involved with Playwrights
Horizons?

WASSERSTEIN: Yes, I just did a benefit for them. And
they had me and Chris and Bill Finn do events in
different parts of the new theater on 42nd Street. And
they gave me the bathroom and I thought to myself,
"After all of these years here I am back in the bathroom
doing a production."

HYLTON: You won the Pulitzer in 1989. How much
do you feel that contributed to future success for you?

WASSERSTEIN: It's funny, but after I won I got
worried about how to follow up the play. It's difficult in
some ways. There's nothing bad about it. It's a
wonderful thing to have achieved. I think in reality
winning the Pulitzer gets my plays read. I don't think it
gets them produced.

HYLTON: What would you tell a young playwright just
starting?

WASSERSTEIN: In terms of young playwrights what I
always tell them is, "What is important is to get involved
with a theater." The theater that you get involved with
does not need to be Playwrights Horizons now. It's
better, in many ways, to be involved with the Playwrights
Horizons of then because you are with a community of
people who are starting something. You become
emotionally invested in that theater. They'll let you
perform. Just get your foot in a door. That is what
matters.

CHRISTOPHER DURANG

Chris Durang was born in Montclair, New Jersey in 1949. He earned his B.A. from Harvard University and his M.F.A. from the Yale University School of Drama. Chris won Obie Awards for his plays <u>The Marriage of Bette and Boo</u> and <u>Sister Mary Ignatius Explains It All For You</u>. He has also received a Drama Desk Award Nomination for his play, <u>Betty's Summer Vacation</u> and a Tony Award Nomination for Best Book for the Broadway play, <u>A History of The American Film</u>. Chris currently co-chairs the Playwriting Program at the Julliard School in New York City with Marsha Norman.

Chapter Three

Night, New Jersey

HYLTON: I want to start by mentioning your website, christopherdurang.com For anyone interested in learning about your publication history or really anything about your plays it is a fantastic resource.

DURANG: Well it's interesting because some part of me became a perfectionist as I was doing it. Or maybe perfectionist is the wrong word. But regardless, I could feel it becoming more and more elaborate as I was coming up with the site. It partially came about because I was getting a lot of letters from college students asking for information for either a play they were doing or a paper they were doing on me. I was flattered they were doing a paper on me but when I would do research on myself, one of the main things that would come up was a site about a production of an old play of mine that I co-authored with Albert Innaurato. It was a six-year-old production of The Idiots Karamazov. And I was surprised that was the first thing that popped up. And it was a really obscure play of mine.

HYLTON: It was the first one you did at Yale as I recall.

DURANG: Yes it was. Anyway, I decided I wanted to make it so people could find more information on me in one place.

HYLTON: It's a great resource. From what I have heard it sounds like your mom played a role in your involvement in theater and drama.

DURANG: Yes, I think that's true. She was very interested in theater and enjoyed it a lot and went to theater in Jersey and on Broadway. So it wasn't a constant topic, but it was discussed. I am a little baffled as to why I got so involved in it at such a young age. But I think her enjoyment of theater did play a role in my interest.

HYLTON: And the first play you did at Yale, <u>The Idiots Karamazov</u>, was written while you were in the program with Wendy Wasserstein?

DURANG: Yes. I became very good friends with many of the people in the program at Yale. My first year I became very close with Sigourney [Weaver] and also Albert Innaurato. In my third year Wendy Wasserstein came. And she was, sort of, the first new close friend I made there since my first year. And then I ended up staying an extra year at Yale. I wasn't in school anymore. But initially I was hired to act in two plays at Yale Rep, which was exciting for me. And when that was over, because that only took about two months, I just didn't have the stomach or courage or money to go to New York yet. So I stayed in New Haven and worked, wrote, and hung out with Wendy.

HYLTON: She loves you so much and speaks so highly of you. She was saying that I should ask you about a summer you two were working together.

DURANG: I think she's referring to a summer that she and I both stayed at New Haven. We both needed to make money and we were watching out for one another to get jobs. And she found jobs for both of us in doing this thing called "coding." It was computer coding. It was a room of fifteen of us and for roughly eight hours a day we went through and read forms that were filled out by students in the medical school. Our job was to code these forms so that the data could be analyzed. And it was about American students' views on foreign medical students. It was an odd job because you could do parts of it without thinking too much. Other parts you had to focus a bit because it was dealing with essay questions. We just sort of giggled at how silly it was, as she said, "summering in the Havens." New Haven has never been too nice of a town.

I had access to my first car at that point. And somehow there was a small airport in New Haven. And we discovered that the airport had this little luncheonette that we liked. And we would drive to the airport to go and have milkshakes. So, when Wendy was leaving, well she had a lot of plants in the apartment, and I had this small Toyota Station Wagon. Well, I drove her and her plants down to New York. And I remember having this very dark joke with her, because we both would have our depressive moods. And the airport was near the Long Island Sound. And I said to Wendy, "Wouldn't everyone be surprised if you just packed all of you plants up into my car and then we drove into the ocean." So we started to imagine Howard Stein, the head of the playwright program, who was a very warm fellow and liked both of us, but had this very funny staccato way of speaking saying, "Chris Durang… Wendy Wasserstein…with her plants in the car… drove into the ocean… Tragic! Tragic loss!" Wendy and I did have fun together.

My friendships were very significant for me while I was at Yale. I had a good time at Yale. I liked how much of the production work was as encouraged as classwork. I was fortunate getting into Yale.

I loved going to Harvard in my undergraduate years, but I was in a deep depression. And I had periods of snapping out of it, and other periods when I didn't snap out of it. But it was a tough time. I was in a much better frame of mind when I got to Yale. And I really loved reading and working with the other students at Yale. And one of the nice things about it was that people like Howard Stein really encouraged you to put your plays on. Many students were upset that you were not guaranteed productions. But I chose not to get angry with that. And I thought if you befriended the directors, and if you were like me and did comedy, you could have things done every weekend at the Yale Cabaret. You'd have a chance, because there was a different show there every weekend. Though, initially, you were looked at rather suspiciously when you were new. You had to win people over. But I kind of rose to that challenge. I was in a good frame of mind at Yale, very positive.

I put on a lot of my plays, and then began being asked to be in other peoples' plays because the acting students worked so hard that you couldn't always find actors to be in your plays. So sometimes the non-acting majors were asked to be in people's play too. I had a really good time doing that.

You had to take this one class at Yale in Theater History. And it was taught by this world famous theater historian. But he never published a book of his stuff. So there was no text. You had to go to every lecture and you had to take notes. And the other thing I didn't like about the class was there were six to eight exams every year. And the tests were really fact and date specific. And I never had been asked to memorize dates in college. It really didn't get me in the mode of learning, but of memorizing, which seemed dumb. So for my first two years I would take it for a couple of months and then drop it saying to myself, "Oh, God I can't take this." And I'd think, well, it's a three-year program. I might leave before it's over. So the second year Howard Stein said to me, "You know, we really like your work so we're not going to throw you out. But if you don't pass this class, we can't give you the degree." So I thought, thank you for the clarity.

So when Wendy came, I thought I have to pass this class because I don't want to go through three years and not get this degree. So I said to Wendy, "Would you study with me and can we both try to pass this class together? Because I can't do it on my own." I think the more studious people really liked it, in fairness to the teacher. I was not in the mood to memorize these facts. And since Wendy was fun we'd stay up all night the night before the exam and make mnemonic devices to remember the facts.

HYLTON: I imagine you still probably remember all of the mnemonics, but not what they stood for.

DURANG: Exactly. I remember there was a play called Gorbeyduct Gorbodoc and it was written in 1565. Probably, I do not remember the actual date. And so we made up Gorbeyduct Gorbodoc sounds like Gorbey Doll Gore Vidal. And in order to remember we decided that when Gorbey Doll Gore Vidal was forty-two and in sixty-five he had an affair with a fifteen year old boy. So that was how we remembered the year 1565. I guess nowadays that seems a dark joke, though after all it is fictional. Sigh. But we spent lots of time coming up with these sorts of silly things and finally got through the course. And, significantly, passed it. It was fun and tolerable because Wendy and I did it together.

HYLTON: Tell me a little bit about your involvement with Marsha Norman in the playwrights program at Julliard.

DURANG: We came in during the second year of the program. First of all, it started from this grant that was given by the Lila Wallace Readers Digest Foundation. It was given to Julliard for purposes of playwriting. At that time Julliard was still primarily an acting program. So the previous head of the theater department used the money for grants to different playwrights to be in residence and to write plays. Actually Tony Kushner wrote an early draft of Angels In America through that program. And then when Michael Kahn came in, he decided he wanted to have an actual playwriting program. So I'm not sure how it started as a dual professor program but it started with Terrence McNally and John Guare who taught as Marsha and I do, jointly at the same time, in the same room. And I think their first class was just five students. Both John and Terrence chose not to go on with it. I gather they just either had mixed feelings or just had too much work of their own going on that time.

So Michael Kahn asked Marsha Norman if she would like to work on it. And Marsha asked me if I'd like to do the program with her, which was a surprise to me. I had known her for many years to say hello to but not known her terribly well. Although we had gotten pretty friendly because we were on the Young Playwrights Selection Committee for several years together. So she asked me and at first I said, "Yes." And then I called back like two days later and said, "You know I just am worried about teaching. When I've done it in the past I never felt terribly comfortable with it. What happens if I don't like the students' work? What if it drains me and I find I do not do any of my own work?" So I was really calling her up to get out of it. Then she said a really smart thing, at least for me psychologically, which was, "Well, why don't you do it for six months and if you really hate it you can quit." And I said, "Oh, ok."

So that was the first class, which was Steve Belber, David Auburn, Kira Obolensky, and Julia Jordan. And basically Marsha had already chosen them. Marsha let me read their scripts and a few others but I was coming in pretty late to the whole process. I liked the choices she made, so I just said "good choices." I also worried, what would it be like to co-teach. I didn't think that I'd actually ever been in a class where people co-taught. Anyway, that first year ended up being such a positive and happy experience. I found that Marsha and I worked and clicked as a "team," maybe because we knew we were approximately the same age and started out our careers at the same time. We found we were deferential to each other in a polite and normal way. We worked well together.

And what's funny is [Marsha and I] are really rather similar in our tastes in theater – we're both old-fashioned in that we like and want plays to have characters and plot. We're not drawn to just a "language play." However, our approaches and manners of expressing ourselves come from very different perspectives. And I feel like it is probably interesting for the students, and also good because they get if not quite two different opinions, they get two opinions that are similar but have different nuances to them. And there was just the sense that she and I found a nice balance between us. Somewhere during the year I started to describe our teaching relationship as us doing our version of Nick and Nora Charles. After a while there was a playfulness that was in the room that was fun. It's still very comfortable, but now I've become more genuinely a friend of Marsha's. I'm very fond of our relationship.

HYLTON: Would you please tell me about your program at Julliard?

DURANG: Well, we have a weekly seminar where the students bring in work, we read it aloud and discuss it. Then the playwrights are supposed to do a couple of readings a month. Sometimes it's one. Sometimes it's two. Basically, I think the two things that are unusual about our program at Julliard are that there are two of us working, teaching simultaneously. And also, and this was similar to Yale, we have these bi-monthly "labs" in which we have access to the acting students at Julliard. They read the plays aloud, which is so helpful to the writer. And that was one of the things I just loved at Yale in my study when I was there. We had this class called "Playwrights Workshop" that the writers and actors were assigned to take. And that's actually how I got to be friends with Sigourney Weaver, because we were in the same year together. And you would bring in either a full-length play or a full act. The actors would rehearse a tiny bit beforehand and then would read it aloud. And the actors both at Yale and Julliard tend to be very talented as well as wanting to learn and stretch their craft. So I find that for a playwright to have consistent access to talented actors to read their work aloud is both pleasurable, and a great learning tool. And the actors learn how to approach a new script that no one's ever done before.

[When I was at Yale] even though I valued the classes where I was with other writers and we sat around and talked about the work, I found the other writers frequently to be rather intellectual and stuck on telling you how they would write [your play], which isn't helpful. I found that the actors had more practical questions. [For example] an actor would say "I don't quite understand what's happening in this scene" and [for a writer] that's important to know. Actors would be coming from a place of trying to find the motivation, or the activity, they are supposed to be playing and just not being able to. And as a writer and an actor I realized that, "Oh, there's a problem there." And this was something that would rarely be as helpfully articulated by another writer.

There was a writer at Yale with me who wrote a lot like Harold Pinter. There was this quiet, unspoken seriousness and ambiguity going on in his work and I found when he would give feedback to me, and to others as well, it would be more to suggest how he would write [my play]. That was frequently not very useful. Marsha and I, along the years, have said we try to avoid telling the writer how to fix his or her play. First of all, that's hubris. But beyond that, we want to tell people, "This is a place where we have an issue" or "This is a place where we loved it, but it got a little lost later." And then if the writer feels that we've identified a place where there's a problem, then it is up the writer to go home and solve it. We do not want to tell them what to do or how we'd solve it. I think there are writing programs where people get into telling each other what to do. We do break our promise from time to time, but it is normally inadvertent and we really try to keep true to that rule.

HYLTON: So you don't break out a text book with your students?

DURANG: Well, no but Marsha does think more theoretically than I do, which is interesting for me to be around. And she'll say "Every good play has only one protagonist. You can't have two protagonists." And I'll sort of think and go, "You know, I would probably say *most* good plays have only one protagonist. However, Marsha's right, when there's one strong protagonist that you follow, it can be very powerful." But no, there are no hard and fast rules. I find when plays break the rules, that can be fun for me, especially when I was younger. But as I've worked with Marsha, and also grown fatigued with too much unenjoyable experimentation, I do value older rules like "you must have one protagonist." I have a new play (Miss Witherspoon), we've done a couple of readings of it, and the main protagonist character is so clearly the main protagonist that it's really indeed quite powerful. It's so clear to the audience we are following that person's story. And when that person's story or journey gets solved or completed, then the play is over.

Anyway, I was starting to say that the other part that is very important about Julliard is the access you have to the actors. It adds that glimmer of production. Plays are meant to be performed aloud, live. Though we do read the plays around the tables ourselves as well. And depending on the year sometimes we have very good readers, other times we have a mixture of good and not so good readers. Every so often we have years when the writers tend to read the plays better than the actors. Though most of the time the actors tend to do a very good job and it's very helpful.

The second year tends to usually include a production to which many student actors are attached. Marsha is very strongly in favor of not doing many rewrites, particularly if it is coming from the actors or perhaps even more from the directors. It was based on a few experiences we had at Julliard where student directors were testing their talents at trying to shape the play. And we found that, depending on the personality of the playwright, many [playwrights] became too anxious to please and really started to lose what had been at the core of their play. And so that is a danger.

We sometimes like to encourage the writer to stop rewriting the first two scenes endlessly, and push onward to a full draft, and then go back to rewriting and reshaping. On the other hand we had a play written by a playwright that both Marsha and I are very partial to, named Jennie Schwartz. And she is writing a play totally intuitively. We kept trying to get her to slow down and get an ending. And every time she had to go back to the beginning, she would expand that earlier material out. And after a while we realized we have to let her do it the way she wants to do it. And she did do a lot of rewrites during her rehearsal, but she kept bringing them into class. And the rewrites kept being really good. And they did not come because the director said, "I think you need a scene in a bowling alley." But the playwright was saying to herself that it wasn't really done yet. We were thrilled with the rewrites she did. So you can't just write these rules in stone.

But we have found at Julliard that some students can get lost in the rehearsal process either by willingness to please or being so open minded. We try to get people not to forget their initial impulses. And this is, of course, also subjective. It's never written in stone. Marsha would tell people that we don't want a lot of rewrites done in rehearsal. I'd end up mentioning the logical exceptions: "But if you are in rehearsals and realize that something is wildly wrong and suddenly realize how to fix it you don't want to stop that either." And sometimes that can be about exposition, not giving the audience the information they need at the right time. But I knew where Marsha was coming from in her attempts to try and stop that going overboard of rewriting in rehearsal.

HYLTON: From the history I read of you, I saw that you frequently have others direct your work. How do you approach those relationships now?

DURANG: I think when I was at Yale I learned a lot about how to approach working with actors and directors. And I found that with directors there were recurring pitfalls in my work -- , and again it's because it has a comic tone that it's hard to hit. And, early at my time at Yale I found good directors who would push it too far toward the camp. And I think Sigourney helped me in this regard because she has some sort of innate realism even in the work she's doing in exaggerated comedy. I think that psychological grounding she brought to me work and to comedy in general is a very good thing.

Matter of fact at Yale I think there were two actresses who were very influential for me. One was Sigourney and the other was an actress named Kate McGregor-Stewart. Kate has a talent like Bette Midler. She has red hair like Midler, and she is innately exaggerated as a redhead comic performer. And like Bette Midler she's coming from a true place so the exaggeration works for her. Sigourney comes from a more realistic place and when she acted in some of my more outlandish plays, it could be really funny when she'd just say something very seriously. And she would be very funny by letting the line do the work and be funnier. She wouldn't exaggerate, it was her truthful simplicity that let the moment or line be funny. I was interested to see that there were these two ways to do it, to play my comedy.

And later I would see that there were people out there who did not have that innate gift for exaggeration that, say Kate had. But they'd try to force an exaggerated style on themselves, and it just didn't fit. They would've been better instead doing Sigourney's route of being truthful (though adding in comic timing which, alas, is mostly instinctual.)

Rather, others would have to come in and realize that they had to be more exaggerated for my play. And they would come in and do it but it would really be kinda pasted on. And it would not be as funny or sort of off-putting and you'd get tired of it. So it's been an interesting process for me. I have to say in terms of my learning how best actors should act my kind of exaggerated world, it's been very interesting having auditions. Some very good actors come in and my material doesn't fit them, even though they're talented. It's just a tonal thing they don't have in their bones. And then you'll be surprised when someone comes in and every single line they say sounds exactly right. They make you laugh and the role just fits them. When Dianne Wiest auditioned for <u>Beyond Therapy</u>, she was like that. Every single thing she did was truthful and hilarious. And I also found that it's hard to know in advance but different directors are able to guide and find that balance of comedy and seriousness. Which is not in all of these plays.

Over the last five years I've said over and over to my students that when they come in and have a reading go well, I'll say, "The reading was terrific." Then they will come back and have done rewrites and they will have changed the scene, they have not just done small adjustments. Or they'll have a first draft I think is terrific, and then they'll come back and have changed it substantially. I will sometimes have trouble and will miss the first draft. But I'll tell them that I'm pretty suspect because I have a tendency to like first drafts and then I have difficulty valuing it when they change it immediately. So if everyone else in the room likes the new version, [they] should keep it. But sometimes I might be right about the wisdom of first drafts. Sometimes your first impulses are very good. First impulses include your first feelings about what you want to be writing about. But I'm aware that one of the things I do with my own writing is that, when I do a reading and it goes well and then I'm later rewriting the draft, I will sometimes go, "Well, this went well in the readings so I am going to leave it alone. And this did not go well so I'm going to focus on that." And about seventy percent of the time I think it goes fine. But other times I think it leads me to not reevaluate things I should.

A play of mine called <u>Sex And Longing</u> was a public failure, although the actors were very good and sections of it were very good. I had two readings of it and the first reading was like four hours long. I thought it needed radical shaping and cutting, but it clicked in the end. Over all, I thought the long version went very well, was funny, and kind of powerful at the end. And then the second reading there were wonderful things, but it didn't quite click together as much. But I thought in rehearsal I would be able to figure out what will work and what won't. And I assumed I'd recapture what seemed to work in the first reading, and save the good stuff, and cut the bad, and shape it. But my rewriting didn't solve things. I think a lot of Act One and Act Two were good, but Act Three really lost the audience. As a whole it didn't work.

And some parts were not the script. The set in particular was problematic. The first scene takes place in a loft sitting on a bed. Sigourney's character sat on a bed and the other character sat in a chair. And the director asked me if he could cut the chair and put the guy on the floor. And I said, "OK." And then when we I saw it, it was the kind of set that was not realistic. So it was like a black void. And Sigourney sat on a mattress with a white sheet on it. So you weren't sure it was a bed and you weren't sure if it was a room they were in, or whether it was in some Samuel Beckett world/void.

And the first couple of weeks of previews I watched it. But sometime early on I said, "Can we give the bed some pillows and try to make it appear more like a bed?" And the director said, "No." I don't know that it would have fixed it. But it might have helped a little bit. Because it seemed like she was sitting on a platform rather than a bed. And the opening was sufficiently strange in dialog that it would have been helpful to know they were in a room. And not in a void. And when she went outside into the street the director didn't have her put shoes on. And I gave him a note about it, but he wouldn't change it. But you thought, "Why is she barefoot out on the street?" It became too unrealistic, too unlikely, or made her too crazy. I made her crazy enough, we didn't need more. So, on and on. Blah, blah, blah. That was one of my few unhappy experiences with a director, although he was very talented, and he has since then died.

HYLTON: Do you have any interest in directing your own material?

DURANG: No, I usually have been fortunate enough to have good experiences with directors. And that director, I just spoke of, directed me two other times as an actor and I had a very good experience with him those times. I think it was a difficult play and I think he had a darker vision of it for the play. Marsha, in retrospect, said she thought that the director failed to bring a warmth to the play that was necessary. It was very cold. And I think she's right. Visually it was cold. It's so interesting what happens in careers. We were all thrilled that Sigourney was going to do it. And it was going to be done at a very cozy theater with only a few hundred seats. Although Sigourney had scheduled to do the film Alien 3, the movie company gave her four and a half months to do this play. We were to have a month and a half of rehearsal and then two and a half months of performing the play. But of course soon after we went into rehearsal the movie company reneged and said, "Well you have three and a half months but not four and a half months."

So, with the large number of subscribers for Lincoln Center, and knowing that there would be a lot of interest in seeing Sigourney, they couldn't get everyone in to see it in the amount of time if we stayed in the intimate Mitzi Newhouse Theatre at Lincoln Center. Which was something that happened when Robin Williams and Steve Martin did Waiting For Godot in the same theater under previous management. The run wasn't long enough to get everyone in, and, thus, there was a lot of anger amongst the subscribers. So Lincoln Center had presented shows at the Court Theater on Broadway in the past, in limited runs as part of its subscription. So there it was in a Broadway house, although it wasn't really a Broadway show.

I thought it would be fine [at the Court Theater] and they were going to do a play by Wendy [Wasserstein] later in the season in the same way at the same theater. But the critics in their reviews all complained about this, and felt that my loony, odd play was being presented as a Broadway play and they thought that Broadway was the wrong place for it. It was too experimental for Broadway they said. I think those cranky reviews were particularly unlucky and, although I never read them, every now and then I will come across one of them and see some line and go "Oh!" with dismay. Though I came to get their point that using the Broadway house gave the wrong aura to the play. And with Betty's Summer Vacation, I made certain to do it in the smaller space of Playwrights Horizons, since it too was very off-beat.

Oh, another thing about using directors rather than trying to do it myself. My late agent, Helen Merrill was a great agent and very supportive of her clients and she tended to encourage me, as a writer, to involve directors. She felt that directors brought an extra perspective that you wouldn't have. And the times that I've done directing -- , I've done a couple of one acts at Yale and a couple of staged readings at other festivals, -- it's been very hard to do and very exhausting. A director never gets a break at rehearsals. A set designer comes up for questions to the director. The writer gets to zone out more.

I think I can be articulate with actors, but over the years I've found that eighty percent of the directors I've worked with are fine with me giving the director and actors very explicit notes about, "I think the actor should not do this part this way" or "I loved what they did last week, but now they've lost the innocence and it's not funny anymore," etc. etc. And the director will usually say "I agree" or "I didn't think of that." Some of them will allow me to talk directly to the actors. If I do that, I will make a point of speaking to the actor and say, "The director says I can speak with you about this but let's actually have the conversation in front of the director so we all know we are on the same page." I think it's very dangerous to speak with the actors without the director present because there can be all sorts of confusion as to who is running the show then. And so the director and I can both check that the point being made was correctly stated. (Oh, sometimes I see a director give an imprecise note, I see the actor hear and take it the wrong way; and I know I have to just be quiet, and let it run its course. It can always be adjusted at a later time.)

HYLTON: How do you feel about working Off-Broadway versus Broadway?

DURANG: I've been fine with my work being off Broadway. I feel like much of my work has been odd in that it's been offbeat, and yet been on the cusp of possibly being commercial. I think A History of American Film, which was on Broadway, could have been successful, and it almost was. It didn't get horrible reviews and it didn't get great ones. And I realized afterward that it's a joke of a title, but it's a joke you get only after you've seen it. It sounds like a college paper, and yet the show is playful and fun though it actually is a history of American movies. But even so, it sounded like a rather scholarly title and I don't think that helped it any. So I'm fine with being Off-Broadway, although I think I expected more of my stuff to possibly cross over.

Young Beyond Therapy was done Off-Broadway, but was redone later with some really good changes done down the road in the play's last 10 minutes. It had a lovely cast with a young Dianne Wiest. She was in it prior to her Woody Allen days. She was wonderful, as was John Lithgow. It was also David Hyde Pierce's first equity job. And it was a really good production and audiences were really enjoying it. And we got some great reviews but both critics in the New York Times saw it as a big nothing. But they were really damning reviews and they thought it was basically just not funny. And it was basically those critics sitting in an audience of people who were laughing and they weren't. And it wasn't one of those reviews where they actually say that. They were confusing bad reviews to get, because in all the previews the audiences were loving it. Frank Rich's review was all about how talented I was but this play wasn't a success. It was a fizzle he said. An interesting kind of happy revenge for me is that play still makes me money, it's one of my most performed plays, even 25 years later.

After the original production of it there was a production at the Arena Stage in Washington, DC that was successful. I loved the Arena and knew them in the 70s and 80s. My play, A History of American Film, started at the O'Neill and then three theaters wanted to do it as a premiere. My agent talked them into doing it as triple premiere, which back then I don't think had been done before. "Otherwise, you're asking Durang to just chose one of you," she said. "But he is a young guy and he's not making any money and it would be great for him and great publicity for all of you." That was probably about three years after Yale. So I had this triple premiere with the Arena Stage and two other productions. And it was a terrific production. Producers saw the Arena Stage production and basically hired the director and the composer and much of the cast. Unfortunately, on Broadway many things went wrong, but it was a great production at the Arena.

I was really upset about Beyond Therapy, because I thought it was an excellent show and the audience really liked the play. It just felt like it was destroyed by The New York Times. So I was fairly dispirited by that. I think the other thing is that I grew up as a child in the 50's and 60's and, in the 50's in particular, I learned that Broadway was where plays really happened. But again I am fine with it being Off-Broadway. Frankly, it's hard getting things Off-Broadway.

HYLTON: How to do you feel about regional theater?

DURANG: I am thrilled about regional theater. When I was just starting out, the first paid production I got was Williamstown doing a production of The Marriage of Bette And and Boo. And I think I got a royalty of fifty dollars. My agent took five dollars and said she'd refer to it as her Kleenex money. So when A History of American Film got produced in the regionals, I was used to being paid nothing for a play, or fifty dollars. So I think from Mark Taper and Arena Stage, which were large audiences, I got probably about eight thousand dollars total, which was thrilling to me. But it was also the first time I think I realized that as a self-employed person they don't take the taxes out. I saved some of it but when it came time to paying taxes on it I had to pay back out all that I had saved. I suddenly had just about zero in my bank account. So I now realize that when I get a check for ten thousand dollars it's really a check for six thousand dollars. I learned to budget for taxes.

But I think the regional theaters are wonderful. I feel like, and this comes from teaching at Julliard more, during the 70's and 80's there was more openness to new plays. I feel like it's harder for young writers to get their work done now than it used to be.

HYLTON: How did you get your first agent?

DURANG: I have to say it happened in a very lucky way. When The Idiots Karamazov was picked up, and it was something we did as students at Yale, it was like winning the lottery to get Yale Rep to do the work of a student. It was thrilling. We got mixed local reviews, but the New York Times gave us a very friendly review that was quite positive. So later when I came to New York and started to have solo plays done, and since Mel Gussow reviewed it, I would get a reference to that play. It was nice because it was positive.

HYLTON: And Mel was a good person to have on your side back then.

DURANG: Yes, absolutely. And back then he tended to review all of the beginning playwrights. And so he was very ubiquitous. But that was very lucky. So in any case, the agent read the Gussow review of Idiots Karamazov. She knew Michael Finegold, from Yale, and she asked him if I had an agent. Michael said I didn't have an agent. So she wrote to me, which was amazing. So I went and met her and she said she was interested, but basically she said I didn't need an agent right away. But she said she was interested and if I had anything done in the City she'd be happy to come and see it.

I had friends in the City who were directors then. And I would advise people to do this, find directors who like your work and stay close with them.

There was a little theater downtown called The Direct Theater, which does not exist any longer. But they tended to do their plays at eleven at night for no money under the showcase code. And my play was only an hour and the agent came to the play. So I said, "Would you be willing to represent me now?" And she said, "You don't need an agent yet. But if you have any contracts come up then give me a call and I'd be happy to advise." So I became very discouraged by that and plus I'd gotten a couple of interviews with a very famous agent. I said to the guy that I would also be interested in writing TV movies. He said you couldn't just come in and write TV movies. He just thought I was an idiot. And I did a second play, <u>Titanic</u>, with Sigourney in it as well, and that got mixed reviews although Mel Gussow gave it a pretty good review. So a friend with money from Yale decided that he wanted to move the play. So we moved it to Off-Broadway and I called the agent in all innocence and said, "I have this contract, can you help me." And she responded, "I will handle it."

The joke is usually that writers think an agent is going to help them get things produced, but that agents are really just there to "field the offers." And of course it's somewhere in-between because there's no question that the good theater agents have good relationships with theaters. And some dramaturges will tell you that they will earmark scripts coming in from a particular agent that they think are particularly good or have a good eye. And also, my agent's talking the theaters into doing the triple premiere was a big coup for me.

When that play (<u>A History of American Film</u>) did not succeed, my mother was suddenly dying of cancer. So for the next year I was mostly dealing with my mother's illness and it wasn't clear how long she was going to live. I was very depressed. And after she died I started to write <u>Sister Mary Ignatius Explains It All For You</u>. I tried to make it into a full length, but it didn't work. The play was wrapping up faster than I wanted. So I almost didn't finish it. But I said, "No, I'm coming out of a writer's block, I have to finish it."

So I sent it to my agent and she told me that she was just so nervous looking at it because she knew what I had been going through, and I hadn't written a new play in a couple of years. So we submitted it to the Ensemble Studio Theater one act festival. At that point I did not know anything about that one act festival. And they did it and it got such a good review that, after a year, it got moved and was performed at Playwright's Horizons and then got to move to Off-Broadway.

HYLTON: And won an Obie Award.

DURANG: And won an Obie. And that was for the Ensemble Studio Theater production.

HYLTON: It is really a struggle getting work read as an unproduced playwright.

DURANG: It's upsetting. I left out something from the story that is indicative of the situation. It's about perseverance. A friend got into the O'Neill several years before I got in there. I submitted several times and kept not getting in. I still think it's an important place to try and go to, by the way. Back then it was very important. But what I like to tell young writers is that I got into the O'Neill on my fifth try. I got turned down four times. But I am so glad I kept trying.

The friend I mentioned who got in earlier also got an agent from having his play seen there. I asked my friend if I could meet the agent. And he introduced me to her and she said, "Oh, yes, I'd be happy to send some of your plays around." So I sent them on to her and I never heard from her again. I don't even remember her name. Back then I didn't know who anybody was.

In terms of other things I mention to aspiring writers, I can't tell how many of these things are still true but I think applying to contests is good to do because contests (and festivals) are set up to read plays whether you have an agent or not. And applying to the O'Neill was open, which is why a couple of years ago when James Houghton said he was changing it so you could no longer do open submissions we were very upset. Happily he resigned and the next person reinstated the old policy. So the policy is still an open submission one.

HYLTON: What happens when one of your students at Julliard is about to graduate?

DURANG: A couple of things happen. There are pluses to being in New York. Even from the year that John and Terrence did the program, students had an evening that agents are invited to. It is a great idea. Fifteen to twenty minutes of a play by a writer are shown. So the Julliard actors do the staged readings and they rehearse, but it's like a coming attraction type of thing. Usually it's directed by Richard Feldman, who is a wonderful acting teacher at Juilliard, and he does a good job with this evening. Many of the writers have ended up getting agents from this evening. And we advise that usually it's best to choose the beginning twenty minutes from the play, but that's not a hard and fast rule.

The second year of the program happened when all of the playwrights from Auburn's class said they wanted to stay for another year. So in the last few years the actors have been working on these second year project plays and the writers are allowed to invite agents to see their work as well. And Joe Kramer [program director] is very willing to make the calls. And so sometimes someone who did not get an agent the first year has a shot at getting one the second year. So they tend to get agents, but how they get their work done is something else. With the kind of success that Dave Auburn, David Lindsay-Abair, Julia Jordan, and many others of our students have had, I have to admit it seems like many theaters look at Julliard writers with interest. Marsha and I are proud of that.

What I thought for myself about Yale School for Drama was not that it solved my life, but it absolutely meant that a couple of doors would open. It didn't mean that you necessarily got to go through the door, but it definitely at least opened. And something else that was true for me at Yale was the creation of this "Yale Mafia." It seems that people from Julliard band together and create a network for themselves.

HYLTON: Interestingly enough that's the thing that both Dave Auburn and Steve Belber said to me. They both spoke of the network they built with Julliard people and how helpful that was for them.

DURANG: My friend Kristine Nielson just said that she worked with this director and said to him, you have to look at this play by Chris Durang. So having schoolmates and friends recommend you is really nice, especially when you're starting out, but even now it is helpful. I also just must admit that breaking into theater or any form of show business is the hardest thing. And there is not only one path. You just never know.

Another piece of advice is never to be stubborn about one play. If you have a play that you think is destined to be your success but no one is saying yes, put it aside for a while and write another play. The fact that I had such a success with Sister Mary was such a surprise to me. I was surprised because I had been told by teachers that you could never get one acts done. And even if you did, you certainly couldn't make money from them. And that is mostly true, but there are exceptions to every rule. The success of <u>Sister Mary</u> – a play I considered not finishing because it wasn't going to end up being full length – was a life changing thing for me. I made money from an Off-Broadway production and it opened doors to writing screenplays. I got better known, which meant theaters were more open to my work. It was a lucky thing. Though I sure was surprised.

MARGARET EDSON

Margaret Edson was born in 1961 in Washington, DC. She graduated with a B.A. from Smith College and earned a Master's in English from Georgetown University. Her play Wit was produced in New York City, won the 1999 Pulitzer Prize for Drama, and was made into a feature film. Magaret lives in Atlanta where she teaches kindergarten.

Chapter Four

Evening, Atlanta

EDSON: I went to college thinking that I would study theater. But then I got very interested in academics. I didn't take courses in theater other than that first year. I became more interested in classical academics. In high school, at Sidwell Friends School, [in Washington, DC] I read many plays and was exclusively interested in theater.

When I think about it, I would never write anything but a play. I would never write a novel. As a genre it would not be interesting for me to write. I started writing <u>Wit</u> in 1991. I finished writing it and I sent the play to one place and it was rejected. And I was really just crushed. So I didn't do anything with it initially.

Then I said, "Ok, I'm going to get serious about this." So I sent the synopsis and dialog sample out. I did it very systematically. I set up a station in my place and sent my info to a very comprehensive list of people. I'm sure they were all rolling their eyes at the time at my persistence. About half of them asked to see the full script. Some rejections were just form letters and some were really helpful. I don't hold any rancor about the way I was treated. I was treated with courtesy then. I understand perfectly why I was rejected. That wasn't hard to understand at all.

It was a hard sell. I mean there was a pelvic exam on stage and a whole thing about poetry and another bit on punctuation. Its reject-ability was evident. Even the title makes you do work. There was no mystery in the rejection. There was, however, a lot of mystery in its acceptance. So I sent it out and it got rejected.

HYLTON: And you were teaching at that time?

EDSON: Yeah, I was teaching early education in Washington, D.C. at that point. My friend from seventh grade, Derek Anson Jones, was at the first reading of the script in July of 1991. He was working as a secretary at Blue Cross/Blue Shield back then. The first reading of [Wit] was done at my mom's house with my family playing most of the rolls. Derek knew of the play from that reading and helped me push it.

One of the places I sent the unsolicited manuscript [of Wit] was South Coast Repertory in Costa Mesa, CA. That was the only theater, out of about sixty, that was actually interested in the play. So, once the South Coast Repertory decided they were interested in Wit, we did a reading of the play. Most of the time theaters get second stringers for readings. I was very fortunate because they got really talented actors involved in the reading and a great director. In fact, the first production had the exact cast from the first reading in the production. We had very, very talented people.

At that point we corresponded a great deal. The theater wanted to cut some pieces and I fought them on it. I really wanted every single word in there. I think that was mainly because I worked so hard on it and I wanted it to show how hard I worked. So, of course, those scenes I didn't want to cut were the first to go. But the production was very exciting to me. And I believed that they knew what they were doing, at the time, so I felt confident. So I started giving in to some of their requests. It became apparent to me that they were working to make the play work more like it felt. They were not trying to turn it into something different. I think they saw it, perhaps, more clearly than I did. Actually, I'm sure they saw it more clearly than I did. I was probably too close, at the time, to the play.

Derek [Anson Jones] was working with Kathleen Chalfant on [Henry V] in Central Park and he showed her the script, hoping that she'd be interested in acting as the lead. Derek knew Doug Hughes [the director] and passed it on to him. Doug had become the director at the Long Wharf Theater in New Haven. The Long Wharf's second stage has such a rich history. And one of Doug's great concerns, when he went to the Long Wharf, was to rebuild the second stage. So they decided to reopen the Second Stage at the Long Wharf with a version of Wit, which Derek directed. Derek and I [talked] about how few plays he'd directed. And he joked, "This isn't the first play I'm directing. It is, however, the first play I'm directing where the audience is not sitting on folding chairs." I think I said, "It might have been the first play where people actually had to pay for tickets."

So, after two years of nothing, the play was produced in New Haven in 1997. And the run was very successful in

New Haven. I was thrilled with what happened with that production. I figured if nothing ever happened again I would have been completely thrilled still. I was done. But luckily, the producer made some calls.

By that point Carolyn French, at Fifi Oscard Agency, who was involved with people at the Long Wharf, became my agent. So she was circulating it to theaters. The New York Times, which has a few readers, reviewed the Long Wharf production the Friday before it closed. And that was interesting because they didn't have to do that. It was very generous of them. And through that review there was more interest and press.

But even with that we couldn't find anyone to move the production to New York. Even then they were working with all sorts of theaters, but it wasn't happening. And then MCC Theater became very interested and decided to do it in their old place. So Derek tried to think about how it could be done in this room. "I mean we could block off part for the stage. The bedroom could be there." And I just remember saying, "Go ahead." And it happened.

HYLTON: How did you manage your job teaching at the same time? Did you take any time off during the productions?

EDSON: No. I didn't take any time off. I flew up to New York for the premiere after school. I just left after school so that I would get there by the time it was ending. And that worked fine. The flight was fine and the cab ride, except that they took me to MCC and I said, "This is not it." I was thinking, "There is no way my big opening night can be here, in the second floor of a warehouse in the wholesale flower district." And the cab driver said, "This is it." And the group was waiting for me in the doorway.

And at the time it seemed that it was going to be the end and it would not go to Broadway. But it next went to the Union Square Theater Off-Broadway. That theater was rather large, seating around 500 people. The cast and production team stayed the same from the MCC production. There were three main producers who put up the capital for this production. One was Darrell Roth, the other was MCC, and the last was the Long Wharf Theater. So instead of a non-profit losing money for once, two non-profit theaters (both MCC and the Long Wharf) ended up making money on the production. And that was very exciting.

HYLTON: How did your life change after you got the Pulitzer?

EDSON: It got very complicated for a while, but I was teaching all the time. I never took a day off of teaching.

HYLTON: That's unbelievable. Were you involved with Mike Nichols' film version of Wit ?

EDSON: I didn't meet Mike until the day of the opening. We had one short conversation during filming, but it was funny, about our families. I decided not to get involved in the film. They were very warm and cordial with me, but I decided not to be involved. I was curious to see what they would make of it. I didn't think it would be fair to be involved. I didn't think it would be right for me to say, "Yes, you can change that. No you can't change that." They didn't make many changes from my original script though. And they could have opened it up. I mean, I signed over the rights to them so they could have. But they didn't.

HYLTON: I understand you no longer write. Do you still get requests for commissions or work on film or TV?

EDSON: People got the idea by now. The offers stopped coming after a while.

HYLTON: Do you miss being involved in the theater or writing for the theater?

EDSON: I read about the theater still. I like to see what is going on. But I'm not involved in that world any longer. For me productions and writing were two very different things. Being involved in productions is one thing. The writing is a totally different issue. The writing, for me, was such hard work. The productions were so much fun. It was hilarious. And I made so many friends through it. It was so much fun. And part of what made it fun was it was completely unexpected.

I just wrote the play to write it. I didn't think about what strategy I was going to use when I was done to get it produced or what I was going to do with it after. And then all of it happened. It was just fun.

HYLTON: What would you suggest to young, aspiring playwrights?

EDSON: Read a lot. Write a lot. You know the tricky thing about writing a play is that what you are writing is meant to be read out loud. And yet your work is being judged in silence, as it sits on the page. So you have to pay attention to that fact. And yet ultimately you must remember, it must "play."

DAVID AUBURN

David Auburn was born in Chicago in 1970. He received his undergraduate degree from the University of Chicago and later attended Julliard University's Playwriting Program. Auburn's play Proof won the 2001 Tony Award for Best Play and the 2001 Pulitzer Prize for Drama. Ultimately, he adapted the play into a film which was released in 2005. Auburn is also the author of several produced screenplays including The Lake House and The Girl In The Park, which he also directed.

Chapter Five

Afternoon, New York City

HYLTON: How do you feel about working on film versus theater?

AUBURN: In the theater you're very much the author of what the audience sees, and having that control over the final product makes it a much more satisfying medium to work in as a writer. While the movies I've worked on have been enjoyable in some ways, when you work for the studios you're more in the position of a contractor who's called in to do some work on a house -- say a roofer. They need a good roof, they need it not to leak, and they pay you to provide it. But it's not your house. And paradoxically, even though you're part of this huge enterprise, you don't have the pleasure of the day-to-day interactions that you get with theater. You generally write the thing alone, send it to your agent, maybe have a meeting or two, and that's it. Whereas, in the theater you get to have the fun of coming into a room every day with the actors, the director, and the designers.

HYLTON: With that said, do you write from an office or at home?

AUBURN: I go to an office I keep. With small kids at home I find I need to get out of the apartment every day to get work done.

HYLTON: How did you get started in theater?

AUBURN: I was always interested. I acted in community theater as a kid. When I was in high school one of my jobs was working as a stagehand for the local professional opera company, in Little Rock, Arkansas. I actually got paid to be a light board operator and stagehand, which is shocking to me in retrospect. I always spent a lot of time around the theater and always enjoyed it. But I never had any idea of pursing it as a career. I was more interested in politics and government – I was a political science major when I started college. But at the University of Chicago, where I went, there's a long tradition of sketch comedy – the Compass Players, progenitor to the Second City, started there in the fifties. And I joined a student troupe that was sort of a descendant of that group; we wrote and performed sketch comedy revues and took it pretty seriously. I wasn't a bad actor, but I wasn't a terribly good one either and I saw very quickly that in order to come off decently in the shows I'd better write myself some good material. I had grown up listening to Monty Python records and other comedy albums, "Beyond the Fringe" and so on. So I had some kind of feel for the form, and quickly found I liked writing sketches and could do it. Eventually the sketches got longer, and I wrote a one act play, then eventually a full-length play. It was probably a pretty terrible play, but I sent it to some Chicago theaters anyway. No luck.

HYLTON: Did you consider graduate schools for playwriting at that point?

AUBURN: No, I never thought too much about grad school. After college I was planning on staying in Chicago and starting a theater company. I had older friends who had done it; they'd started storefront companies and over the course of a few years built an audience, got some attention from the critics, developed a reputation for their work. They didn't make any money, they worked long hours at boring jobs in order to stage shows in tiny bars and basements at night, but it was nevertheless a very sound do-it-yourself model for how to begin to work in the theater, and it appealed to me.

However, around this time, I randomly saw a poster advertising a screenwriting contest that Amblin Entertainment and Universal were co-sponsoring in Los Angeles. Under the program they supported you, modestly, while you learned to write screenplays. So I submitted my play to that program, on kind of a lark, and I actually forgot about my application. But I got a call about three months later saying I had gotten in.

So I spent a year in L.A. hanging out on the Universal Lot. By the end of the year I had a screenplay. The fellowship ended and I spent six more months in L.A. trying to do something with the script. Nothing happened, and it quickly became apparent to me that if I was going to go broke trying to be a writer I should do it in New York trying to be a playwright, not in Los Angeles trying to be a screenwriter. I missed having a group of people to work with. So I moved to New York.

HYLTON: What did you do to support yourself when you were in New York starting out?

AUBURN: I had a range of jobs. I temped. I typeset the programs for Carnegie Hall. I did a good deal of freelance copy editing. I worked for a documentary filmmaker for a year. I worked in publishing. I did pretty much whatever I could do to pay the bills while I continued to do small shows with friends at little theaters downtown. For two of those years I was at the Julliard School in their playwrighting program, taught by Marsha Norman and Chris Durang. (I was there with Stephen Belber, who I think you interviewed for this book.) And that was hugely valuable. I felt I was getting my feet wet in the "real" New York theater world.

HYLTON: I know that Julliard does not have a formal curriculum, but they allow you to take acting classes if you wish. Did you participate in any of the classes?

AUBURN: Yes, I audited the acting classes and took Alexander technique and a number of other things. But mostly I just wrote my plays. The genius of that program is that it is sort of an nonprogram in a sense. You write your plays, you talk about them with other playwrights, and you see them performed. What else do you need?

HYLTON: What did you submit for your application for Julliard?

AUBURN: I sent in two one-acts I had written my first year in New York.

HYLTON: And these two works you did for Julliard, did you do readings prior to submitting them or did you workshop them?

AUBURN: They had been performed. One had been done in a staged reading by a director friend; another I had produced myself.

HYLTON: What kind of places were you experimenting with when you were self-producing?

AUBURN: They were the type of places that you could rent for a week or a night at a time. Usually some kind of bar with a back room where you could perform, but occasionally a properly equipped 50 or 99 seat house.

HYLTON: What do you feel like you gained from those experiences?

AUBURN: It's how I learned to write. That and doing the sketches. Those experiences gave me a good, basic toolkit of techniques; taught me how to establish a situation, how to establish character; how to set up a joke, and how to diagnose the problem when something isn't working. You learn how actors think, the questions they ask when they approach a text, and how to look at the work from their point of view. I directed many of these myself. I was always impatient and always had a sort of "what-the-hell," trial-and-error approach. You'd put something up and if it didn't work we'd say, "OK, what needs to be fixed?" And we'd try and fix it.

HYLTON: How did you get your agent?

AUBURN: A friend who had directed some of my one acts, was working at the New York Stage and Film Festival one summer. She asked to do one of my plays there. It went well. And the producer of the festival took me aside and said, "How can I help you?" He put me in touch with several agents and I ended up signing with one of them. He's still the only agent I've ever had.

HYLTON: Would you tell me a little about your first full length professional production?

AUBURN: It was called <u>Skyscraper</u>. I wrote the play while I was at Juilliard. It was done commercially Off-Broadway in 1997.

HYLTON: What was it like getting produced on that scale at such a young age?

AUBURN: Exciting. I think I was twenty-six. It was a beautiful production. The reviews were not great, so it didn't run for very long, but overall I was just so pleased to have a decent production of what was, in a way, quite a peculiar play.

HYLTON: So how did it happen that Manhattan Theater Club picked up <u>Proof</u>?

AUBURN: One of their literary managers saw <u>Skyscraper</u> and said "Keep us in mind next time you have something." A couple years later I had written <u>Proof</u>, and I sent it right over.

HYLTON: What's it like now that you've won the Pulitzer? Do you get many commission requests from theaters?

AUBURN: Some, but I haven't taken any. I feel more comfortable waiting until I have a script in hand and then finding someone who wants it.

HYLTON: What about doing blind submissions?

AUBURN: Earlier in my career I made a few. I remember getting the <u>Dramatists' Sourcebook</u> and marking it up, but I never got the sense that mailing scripts blind to strangers was the way to go. It seemed much more useful to develop a community of people and put on shows with them. At worst you'd be producing new work and teaching yourself and having fun; at best maybe somebody in the group would get a break and then drag the rest along with them, or maybe you yourself would be the lucky one.

I think when young playwrights ask about building careers they often worry about the wrong things. For example, I think that the value of an agent early on is vastly overrated. The value of "contacts" in the business is similarly overrated. Now, obviously different things work for different people. But for me the key was to produce myself in whatever grubby conditions I could. Everything came out of that effort.

PAULA VOGEL

Paula Vogel was born in Washington, DC in 1951. Vogel earned her B.A. from the Catholic University of America and a Masters of Arts from Cornell University. She won an Obie award for her play The Baltimore Waltz *(1992) and a Pulitzer Prize for the play* How I Learned To Drive *(1997). Vogel led the graduate playwright program at Brown Univeristy for two decades where her students included Pulitzer Prize winning playwright Nilo Cruz and MacArthur Fellowship winner Sarah Ruhl. In 2008 Paula left Brown to chair the playwriting department at the Yale School of Drama. She is currently Playwright in Residence at the Yale Repertory Theater in New Haven, Connecticut.*

Chapter Six

Afternoon, New York City

VOGEL: I live on Cape Cod in Truro, as well as in Providence and now, New Haven. The year-round population in Truro is a bit more than five hundred. There are wonderful small theater companies on the Cape. There are very good local writers and very good local actors. I once brought in my graduate students to do readings of their work out there. They were honored by these actors.

I spend a great deal of my time with small regional theater companies and my students. I work primarily with graduate writers, who are students who have been out in the world. I would say they range in ages from twenty-three to forty five. We accepted one playwright who entered the MFA program at age sixty-one—as a retired businessman. He went on to see his plays produced in London and L.A., and became an important friend in my life.

I've spent about twenty years of my life working with a theater company in Juneau, Alaska. Juneau has a population of twenty-eight thousand. I have had all of my plays done there first, on a tiny stage with fifty seats. It's there I came of age, in many ways, as an artist. All of my plays were beautifully acted there by people who are fisherman, lawyers for the state, and schoolteachers. So I imagine I actually have a very different view of regional theater than many of the people you have interviewed. I have been inspired by "amateurs;" the emerging and the passionately involved artists who underwrite their lives in theater with day jobs. They exemplify the meaning of "amateur," those who practice their gifts for the love of the art.

People are always surprised by my spending time in Alaska /Provincetown/Providence and are often condescending in that east coast urban inflection: "Oh, you're working on something in Alaska." But I see more writing which is wild and exciting and cutting edge on these tiny stages. I see writers and work that won't be seen by New York for ten years--I see them first. I see attempts to try something new and even the shortcomings are thrilling. All from writers and artists whom New York theater folks might characterize as amateur. It is crucial that we share information on possible day jobs one can have that subsidizes the love of writing plays.

One of the day jobs of course is film writing. For myself, I find teaching a more exciting day job. I think it is stimulating to see how ten minds approach the same topic and write ten different plays. I think [the playwrights'] frustration, anger, and risk-taking keeps me honest in a way that film writing will not. So I make somewhat less money [teaching] but I actually get much more enjoyment out of the experience. And I very much prefer being a regional theater playwright. I lived in New

York for years. I don't make money when my plays are done in regional theater. But what I do get is a very intensive discussion by audience members and critics who are not treating it as one more fashion show with a jaded palate, positioning themselves against each other. I get audience members who are living in towns where it's mandatory to know your neighbors for the health of the town. [These people] wrestle with the darkest themes in a way that makes me feel I am not alone.

HYLTON: I spoke with one of your former students, Nilo Cruz, about his experiences with <u>Anna In The Tropics</u>. Would you consider doing a play on Broadway?

VOGEL: No one has put my plays on Broadway. It's not a matter of me considering doing it. The playwright doesn't produce the play. Even though <u>How I Learned To Drive</u> has been done all over the world, I was told that it was an Off-Broadway play rather than a Broadway play: it wasn't, I was told, "universal." And so Doug Aibel, who produces for the love of theater, did me the honor of producing it in the Vineyard Theatre with 135 seats. I do think it's a matter of gender in my generation.

I am the first openly lesbian playwright to win the Pulitzer. I am not saying I am the first lesbian to win the Pulitzer. I'm saying I am the first out lesbian to win the Pulitzer. I really don't know if I'll ever crash through the glass ceiling of Broadway. But I've seen the playwrights I taught cross that line: I crossed my fingers on <u>Anna In The Tropics</u>. It was a miracle that a play by a Latino playwright would make it and win on Broadway. Nilo's work cannot really be categorized. Nilo has his own unique language that he's created. It's a blessing now to see Quiara Hudes, whom I worked with five years ago, become the first Latina writer on Broadway. It was a great day when Suzan-Lori Parks was produced as well.

It's not the content of the individual play. It's the identity of the playwright that keeps barriers up. As welcome as it is to see that Nilo, Quiara, and Suzan-Lori have broken through, I think there's very much a notion of keeping the "Great White Way" white. And I think we're turning our back on some of the most important things we learned during the 1960s about this art. We have been facing the most impoverished commercial theater that I've ever seen in my life. It's ghastly. And I don't need to tell you that. But what a writer has to figure out is what they can do for a day job that will allow them to pay the rent and to keep their spirit intact. (Note: I said the above in 2006 during the last two awful years of the Bush administration. I am much more hopeful about our reevaluating our priorities as Americans; opening access to the arts, and valuing the arts).

The goal for anyone who writes for theater, for the love of it, should not be to get awards or really to make large sums of money. The goal is not to get a Pulitzer. The goal should be to be able to work on your own voice. You want to grow, to have the ability to try different things and take risks, to respond to the community, [and] to respond to the world. To be an artist is a very expensive habit: artists in this country are underwriting their addiction to their art form. But I know that when I write a new play someone will eventually do it. It may not get done on Broadway. But hopefully it will get done, and I get the opportunity of continuing to work.

I think there are economic reasons why [Doug Wright's play] I Am My Own Wife, which is a wonderful show, can be on Broadway. It's essentially a one-person show. For non-musical plays written by Americans, it comes down to financial considerations. But many writers should be on Broadway who are not and will not be (and why would <u>Wit</u> not be done on Broadway?) For myself, I can hope that I will be lucky enough to sit next to one of my ex-students when they are on Broadway. That may be the closest I can get to Broadway.

I am enjoying experiencing Sarah Ruhl take the theater world by storm and inspire the next generation of writers. It is very exciting for me. I've witnessed an incredible group of younger writers rising in the past two decades. What I worry about is that the cultural editors and many critics are giving us a message that new plays and younger writers are not important. Now, in regional theater that is not true. Now, for example, a play could be done somewhere in New York. This new play might get a couple of inches of column if one is lucky, or simply appear on-line. And then with a bad review from the New York Times, the future of that new play may be over the next day. On to the next.

Or we can take that same play and go to Seattle, or Portland, San Francisco or Minneapolis where there is an actual discussion in the community. People sit and think about the play and respond to it. That scenario is what I want. It is not money or Broadway. I want to be aligned with an environment that responds and challenges me.

If we don't win this argument over the importance of the new play and the American playwright there is going to be nothing but what I call "Gladiatorial Entertainment For The Empire." (Again, please note: I am more hopeful as now. We shall see what happens in an Obama administration!) I'm not worried about my generation of playwrights. I'm worried about the generation twenty years down the road. That's what I am scared about. That's what keeps me up at night. And like you say, there's no one way of making it.

I've been writing plays since I was what, fourteen. I finally caught a break with <u>Baltimore Waltz,</u> which was my nineteenth play. I was finally discovered at age forty-five in a hundred and twenty-five seat theater. I'm very lucky.

The object of society should really be to keep the doors of theaters open and accessible, as our public libraries should be. If you have a hundred and twenty five seats, you need incredible luck and vision to survive in New York's climate. It's almost an impossibility that the Vineyard Theatre continues to produce stimulating work season after season, with a small staff and a tiny space. So new writers are saying, "I'm not going to New York. I'm going back to Austin. I'm going to Seattle. I'm going to Minneapolis."

HYLTON: Given your attitude towards experimentation and avant-garde theater I wonder what kind of program you expose your students to at Brown. Take for example, Nilo Cruz or another one of your students.

VOGEL: Well, let me say this first. Nilo Cruz was never a student of mine. I don't teach students. I gather together some people into a room and say to them, "Tell me how you see the world." And I may have questions about their play but I tell them, "You train me how to read your play." Because I am an older generation of playwright and the devices I use in my plays are already somewhat antiquated. If you can train me, you can train an artistic director, and you can train a theater. Train me. And by the way, as I am reading your work I'll tell that playwright, "You know there was an interesting German playwright who lived in 1930 and you might like his work. There are some similarities and it might be interesting for you to read his work. You know, there's something very interesting about the world you create. And by the way, I'm assuming that you've read David Greenspan." So, really I see my role as being a matchmaker. I try and find playwrights who are already artists and introduce them to other writers, directors, literary managers and theaters.

I have a brain trust of playwrights. They are already on their way. What I am doing is giving them the ability to have a fully funded space and I see them as teachers for myself. We call them students so that Brown University will pay the bills for two years of time where I expect them to come out with about five to six new works in that two-year period. I expect them to use the time to stockpile first drafts that they can work on. (Note: having left Brown for Yale School of Drama, we now support writers for three years. What a luxury to have that extra year of time). I expect that anyone I am working with is an artist and I treat them as artists. So I don't fit into the "Here are your thirty-six credit hours, do them" sort of path. Yale, like Brown during my time there, is extremely rigorous. It's going to take up many hours a week. We will have conversations where I will find out what you've read and what you haven't and what I haven't read that you've read. I'll find out if you've acted. "You haven't? Well, guess what? You're acting in the next directors' showcase next weekend. Have you directed? No? Well, you better direct. By the way, I want you to know how to run the lights board. By the way, I want you to produce."

I try to make them look at every angle. "Oh, yes, and you must take screenwriting. And what do your screenplays look like? And have you written any poetry? Have you thought about a cross genre work?" On day one I say to the students, "Your greatest responsibility is to say 'No' to me." Any suggestion I make you should respond, "No, and here's why." I think that is important because it will help playwrights make stronger choices. "Your greatest responsibility is to your own voice."

When I was creating the program [at Brown], I thought to myself, "What is it that playwrights need? What is it that I needed and I never got? How do I create a program that is actually driven by playwrights as playwrights? Not a program driven by directors or actors. But driven by playwrights writing for the theater, exploring issues playwrights face. How do I give not only money but more importantly time and space and saying to writers, "I am admitting you because I love your work. I have nothing to "change" in your work. I have questions to ask you about your work. And those questions may lead you to rethink your plays. I will tell you what is in my heart. I will tell you the emotions that your work stimulates in me."

I want to talk about it because there are things that I do not understand. "The hair on the back of my neck stands up when I read your work. I think you're talented. Make me uncomfortable. Here's the stage. Here's a hundred dollars I can give you per production. It's amateur actors or student actors. You have three weeks. Show me. And you'll have an audience that will support you. And young people will go home at Christmas time at 18 years old and say to their parents, 'I want to be a playwright' because they just saw and were moved by your work." That's what I'm trying to do.

I think what playwrights need is for someone to hand over the whole theater to them. And to say to them, "Here's the apparatus. Oh, yeah, by the way, you may have to direct the play. Sometimes you have to work with others. But fine, just astonish me. Here's the space." I have seen Nilo Cruz stage his own work on one hundred dollars and produce a carnival, a Mardis Gras, with umbrellas that was as astonishing as anything I've seen done. It's not about money. It's actually about the limits of money. You would think New York has that. But actually it doesn't. So that's why I started this. That's what I wanted to do.

The question is, "What is the conversation among your peers about?" Some things that work for some people don't work for others. When you choose a theater you want to choose one with the proper aesthetic. I can get ten people in a room with nothing in common to respond to their colleague's script and say, "Did that work for you? Interesting. That's thrilling. How did you do that? Why did you do that?"

In the theater, I've never seen a complete failure. I've never seen a complete success. I don't think they exist.

The question of whether you direct your own play or not depends on the artist. I think you need to learn how to speak with directors. I think certain artists are director/writers. And that's great. But at a certain point, your art has to become detached from your own person, your own body. Personally, I don't like directing my own work. I like hearing it differently than I heard it in my head. I can't wait till the table work is over, till the actors take over the piece. I can't wait till I can forget who wrote the play. I like that form of out of body experience.

I do think playwrights need to find a way to find their routes. You have to find out what is your own way. It would not be of any use for me to try and imitate Edward Albee, who is extremely effective with his own work, but in an Edward Albee way. I think Suzan-Lori Parks is very effective but in a Suzan-Lori Parks way.

HYLTON: I get the sense from reading your plays that Thornton Wilder was an influence on your work.

VOGEL: I have always loved Thornton Wilder. Many of those writers from the thirties and forties were great because they were not literal minded. I think there is a danger that we have begun to become a very literal minded theater world. Unfortunately, we have lost the ability to use the stage metaphorically or to use the stage as an idea. Sadly, we now insist that we are watching the people as real characters rather than abstractions. The characters on stage are always abstractions. There is no such thing as a real person up there. We refuse to believe this. And that is a dangerous drift. It is the inability to engage in storytelling without insisting it be a literal, material truth. That is really dangerous for a democracy. One of my aims for the next ten years is to look at playwrights who are no longer read and no longer taught. I want to read and talk about the forgotten plays to talk about a time that was so different. Even Shakespeare we've made real, which is crazy. We are losing the "muscle of abstraction." We are refusing to think as a society in anything other than the literal.

There is a very dangerous deterioration that is going on within us as a result of this mindset. When critics say to me, "Well, women don't talk that way." I ask, "Which women?" And I think to myself, "Any woman I create can talk any way she pleases." Why are we insisting on a one to one relation to what we perceive as reality? It's the inability to story tell and know it is a story and engage in a story that is dangerous. It's a defense mechanism. I don't have to feel emotionally moved if I can pick it apart and say, "We don't say that" or "We wouldn't say it that way." Instead we should look at the work and say, "Oh, in this play by Ionesco, called The Chairs, never mind the gap between how I talk and how these two characters talk. In this play…the aged are jumping out the windows and committing suicide because no one is listening to what they are saying."

We don't insist on our literal minded perception of reality if it's a classic. But if Samuel Beckett wrote Waiting For Godot with two guys sitting on a bench doing nothing now, we wouldn't do the play. He might get done at small theaters in Boston and Seattle. But he wouldn't make it in New York. No reviews in the New York Times.

HYLTON: How did you come up with your theory of teaching?

VOGEL: I was rejected by the Yale School of Drama. It made me think of techniques to form a community for playwrights…and alternate ways to forge a career. Now I teach there.

It's fortunate I had an inspired teacher when I was at Cornell who taught me about teaching, about structure, and said to me, "By the way, you're a playwright, don't go into academia."

I started writing a lot, I read lots of dramatic literature and dramatic theory. I basically bounced out of graduate school without a PhD. I came to New York. I starved for seven years. I did a lot of staged readings of my work. I worked for a lot of theater companies where I saw them choose the most mediocre scripts. And the scripts that we all agreed were electrifying, never got done. This was in the late seventies and eighties. I saw brilliant groundbreaking work turned away because it was not commercial enough. I left New York after getting offered a great opportunity by Brown University to design a program.

HYLTON: What are you looking for in playwriting program applicants?

VOGEL: What I am looking for is a critique on stage of our world. And you can do that through realism too. And I've sometimes taken people who are so realistic that my hair stands up straight and I get scared. And you can do it with nineteenth century realism if you really stick to it. You can make David Mamet and Neil LaBute seem sentimental. If you can do it in a way that pushes the envelope, I will take you into the program. If you can think about theater in an abstract way, as a metaphor, as a process that creates emotional meaning, that is what theater it is. I don't care what "ism" they are, what voice they are, what devices they use. As long as a writer makes me look at the world anew....that's what makes me get up each day.

I worry that we are not reading enough as artists in the theater. I teach workshops in many different places with people who dare to try playwriting. With "amateurs." And they do every bit as well as graduate students. And they always teach me something new about how you can look at something. It makes me so excited.

During the last eight years of the Republican reign, I've had a disconnect that I have never experienced before in my lifetime. I know a hundred voices out there all around the country that I've worked with in the last ten years. Vibrant, funny, scary, brave, and then there is the surface of theater I see in New York all too often.

I am feeling very positive and joyous because I know these writers are out there. You won't hear me telling people to go into another field. You will hear me saying "I know there are people out there making theater that is the most dangerous, vital theater I know of, the most human." The thing I think I prize the most is courage. Emotional courage is amazing to display. I think in this country our theaters are getting into a habit of losing their courage because they are not embracing the play world on its own terms and not taking the journey. They are making excuses not to take the journey. "Oh, that's not real. Oh, I don't believe that. Oh, they wouldn't say that. Oh People don't do such things." It's a way of hiding. It's a way of disengaging. Younger writers are not disengaging. They are very, very brave. So, it's this strange thing. There is vibrancy and urgency in the playwrights that I know.

LEE BLESSING

Lee Blessing was born in 1949 in Minneapolis, Minnesota. He was educated at Reed College and the University of Iowa. Blessing's play <u>A Walk In The Woods</u> (1986) was produced on Broadway and was nominated for both a Tony Award and a Pulitzer Prize. He was a playwright in residence at New York's Signature Theatre and has had many plays produced Off-Broadway and in regional theaters. Blessing has also written scripts for film and television including <u>Homicide: Life on the Street</u> and <u>Picket Fences</u>. Lee currently heads the graduate playwriting program at Mason Gross School of the Arts, Rutgers University.

Chapter Seven

Afternoon, New York City

HYLTON: I first became aware of your plays when I saw a production of your play <u>Thief River</u> at the Signature Theatre in New York City.

BLESSING: That theater is pretty interesting because it didn't exist in 1990 and now I think it's the fourth largest Off-Broadway theater in terms of budget. Peter Norton funded the space that they're in, so they named it for him. Jim Houghton founded [the Signature].

HYLTON: I know you have a master's degree in playwriting. I imagine there is quite a bit of benefit in such a program, just in terms of learning the craft.

BLESSING: I actually got MFA's in both in English (poetry) and in Drama. It was at the same institution, over a five-year period. It's been tremendously useful. It helps if you want to teach and much of the way that you can earn any kind of living as a playwright is finding a way to teach it. It gives you a very pragmatic basis. But playwriting, more than any other genres, takes a long time to work. So a master's program is a great place to go and do that without a lot of production issues.

As a working artist you are not an academic and you are not a scholar. You might be, but most people are not. If you get an advanced degree, and this is considered a terminal degree for good reason, you can teach playwriting depending on your background.

HYLTON: It is a terminal degree because there are no doctorate programs essentially?

BLESSING: Exactly. There's almost nothing in this country. There are many doctorate degree programs in theater but not specifically in playwriting. So those who go into it want to be playwrights. Usually when you go out into the real world it's very hard to make a living as a playwright. Even the top echelon people don't make that much money at it. It can be a struggle. It's always an unpredictable life, a very volatile one. When I started teaching at Rutgers one of the real shocks was "Oh my god. They send us a paycheck every two weeks." It had been since 1973 that I was getting a paycheck every two weeks. There was a time where I had four paychecks all year.

HYLTON: You've done work both with film and television as well as work on the stage. How did you end up getting to work in film and television?

BLESSING: If you're lucky people get interested in your work. Not a lot of them. Sometimes you write specs or pitch projects or come up with series ideas. When I was out in L.A. I wrote a cable movie that got made. I wrote a film that got made. I got assignments on series like Homicide and Picket Fences and those sorts of things. It's always nice to know that you can do those sorts of things. They can be financially rewarding.

HYLTON: So how did you get those opportunities? Was it through people seeing one of your productions?

BLESSING: Generally.

HYLTON: Did you have an agent?

BLESSING: I worked with an agent in L.A. and in New York.

HYLTON: Once you graduated how did you go from being a graduate, with a catalog of plays, to getting readings and actually getting work produced?

BLESSING: There is no real track. Basically it has to do with the quality of your writing and/or if what you write smells particularly commercial. That's one motivation. The other is, "Is this a voice I've never heard before?" There are any numbers of entry-level situations. Minneapolis has a great facility called the Playwrights' Center. They have about fifty playwrights hanging around town. And they listen to each other's readings. So people start working their way up through small productions in small theaters. And then you start thinking as a playwright.

You need readings, you need productions, and you need feedback. Then you have to learn how to use the feedback and know what is useful and how to throw away the rest. Those are skills that take a lot of time to master. And you need to be very lucky. The first professional production I had was about three years after I graduated from grad school. I sent that play to my then-agent. The agent wrote back and said essentially that there is no way we could market this play. At the same time I sent it to

Seattle Rep's reading series. Same thing, no interest. I sent it to the Milwaukee Rep, where they knew me, and they also said, "No." And that same script I also sent to the Humana Festival of the Actors Theatre of Louisville. They said, "Oh, we love this. We want to do it." So my first professional production was in 1982 at Humana. The same oft rejected play.

You have to develop a thick skin, because you are going to get a lot of rejections. One of the good things about being a poet was I was used to sending to twenty places and getting many rejection letters. So it was easier in a sense for me. I got very lucky with that show. That was my first regional production. My first production in New York was on Broadway with, A Walk In The Woods with Robert Prosky and Sam Waterson.

HYLTON: I'm interested in your perspective on getting readings done through some of the smaller New York theaters. I know Ensemble Studio Theater does readings and has a young playwright's group called Youngbloods. I know that Naked Angels does Tuesdays at Nine.

BLESSING: Cherry Lane Alternative Theater does something. Playwrights Horizons does things. There are a lot of levels and venues for reading series.

HYLTON: Aside from creating opportunities to teach playwriting, what do you feel is the value in getting the MFA in playwriting towards helping your career as a playwright?

BLESSING: It can be very valuable if it's accompanied by production. At Mason Gross [Rutgers], we do guarantee a production of a one act for each of your first two years. And we're committed to doing a main stage production of the play in the thesis year, the graduating year. Hopefully we'll continue doing that. It is unusual, especially in the New York area. Since we only take two playwrights a year, we can say, "Yes, you will get a main stage production."

HYLTON: And in terms of what a MFA means for a new playwright. Do you feel this will enhance your ability to get your work read and produced by theaters? Essentially, do you feel that theaters will take a student with an MFA in the topic more seriously than one without?

BLESSING: Not the degree itself so much as the experience it represents. One of the things I love about theater is that a play is either compelling or it isn't. And it really doesn't matter who did it. One of my favorite memories is when I was at the Playwrights' Center. One of the guys in that group was a great actor. His was the sweetest, funniest, most joyful character I'd ever met. But he was an actor. Nobody thought he could write. Then one day he started walking around the Center saying, "Hey everybody, I wrote a play. Wanna come around and hear it?" So you can't say no to him since he's the sweetest guy in the world. So he sat down to read this play to us.

And we're like "Oh my god." The play was called 21A, after the name of a bus line. He performed it with a line of chairs and jumped from chair to chair playing every role. It was a one-man play. He started reading this play, and it was extraordinary. It was hilarious. It was really well crafted. You'd hear one side of the conversation early on in the play and then you'd hear the other side of the conversation an hour later and you still had it in your mind. In retrospect, I realized, it was literally the experience of watching a playwright coming into existence in the period of an hour and a half. So it really is merit based. If it works, an audience knows it. If it doesn't work, it doesn't work.

To do theater you really have to get some sort of aesthetic enjoyment out of it and believe in the art form per se because there is no guarantee even if it is well received that it will receive financial success. With film and television you really are going to Vegas so you push every button you can reach. Which is fine. In theater it is more of a constant effort to put something out there, look at the audience reaction, ask yourself what's working and what isn't, relax about getting somewhere, go back and do some more writing and put that in front of people. It's really kind of a step-by-step process. People have to be tremendously patient, because this concept of making it and not making it is off. I don't think that's what it's about in theater. Very, very few people become stars in the New York press. You just want to aspire to be a solid writer who gets his or her work done from time to time.

HYLTON: I know that many playwrights who end up sending their scripts to theaters they found in The Dramatists' Sourcebook end up receiving rejections so fast that it seems they couldn't possibly have had their work read by the theater. Do you feel that a playwright's notoriety or lack of a name has something to do with this?

BLESSING: Well, a lot of these theaters get many applications and many don't have much in the way of a staff to review the work. I've had grad students of mine go to theaters to be that first line reader. It's not an easy job to screen scripts. With theater you're writing something that is for an experience. And neither you nor the reader can really judge how it is going to be experienced by an audience. They can guess. They can have an instinct about it. But you can't be sure until you get it in front of an audience. Certainly they'll look harder at plays by well-known writers, but the play has to speak to them, no matter who you are.

HYLTON: From my experience it is a very confusing situation when you're starting out. Many playwrights I know feel completely blind, stumbling around with no idea of where they're going or how to get there.

BLESSING: It's far more Zen than that. What did they say about Basho? He used to write Haikus on a piece of paper, then fold them into boats and put them in the stream to float away. You have to develop a philosophical nature about it. You have to be doing it for a larger purpose rather than for the sense that it's somehow got to satisfy your career ambitions. I think a writer should focus on writing plays well. Quality writing is what gets noticed, in the end.

HYLTON: In terms of your applications for Rutgers what are you looking for in an applicant?

BLESSING: For the most part I look for people who are not coming straight out of undergrad because it takes a long time to learn how to write plays. It is the most emotional of the literary forums, so that if you have not had time to mature emotionally, and most people in our culture have not, then you need a little time out there dealing with life. "Oh, I have to pay the bills. Oh, I'm alone. Dating? What's that about?" It's better to have dealt with necessity. Plays are about necessity. So usually, we look for people who are a couple years out of undergrad. Last year though, I took someone who was straight out of undergrad. And he was great. So it varies. The first person I took was thirty-four. And then this year a couple of women both in their later twenties, who have been out for a while. Mostly, 95% of it, assuming one has an undergraduate degree and a decent GPA, are the script samples.

How do you write? What do you write? What happens when you write dialog? What you're looking for, amongst other things, is if this person can create interest with every line? Is there something happening in a speech that is more than just that speech? The speech should be doing two things. What is that character saying to that other character? Also, underneath it, not just the subtext of what that character's real motivations are, but underneath that, is the real play, what that author is saying to you as an audience. Why has this author had this character say this speech right now? So you are registering it in all of these senses. There should be compelling tension between those levels in the dialog. And it's mostly subliminal. So I look for that. You can read 100 scripts and many will have completely dead dialog. It may serve a couple of functions, but it doesn't do the whole thing. If twenty of them had great dialog that would be a lot. It's a very mystical process. There is a certain mystical quality to what makes a play work. So, I look for something that is exciting. I want a point of view that I did not walk into the theater holding. If that's there and it takes me somewhere new and interesting, then that is attractive.

HYLTON: What do you try to communicate to your students about playwriting?

BLESSING: Sometimes we don't think with too much focus about what we're trying to do with a play. When you write a poem you write it to evoke some feeling or experience that you had. The writing focuses it. We read it once and have that experience. When you write a play it should be like that. You shouldn't think, oh, well, I have these characters on stage and they're saying things to one another and I have to care about what they care about- what's their point of view? They only exist because you have something to say to an audience. The audience are the only people who are for the first time experiencing the play, after all. The actors are there to deliver it but they are not what the play is about. The work preexists production.

HYLTON: What advice do you have for writing the play?

BLESSING: Start with the end of the play and work backwards. From the beginning of writing you have to know what the end of the play is going to be so that you can know what should go into the play. Nothing can be in a play that is not essential. A play cannot be a minute more than it needs to be. You don't want an extra character. It's not a digressive medium. It's not a novel.

ALFRED UHRY

Alfred Uhry was born in 1936 in Atlanta, Georgia. After graduating from Brown University he moved to New York City where he started his career by writing for theater. Uhry won the Pulitzer Prize for his play <u>Driving Miss Daisy</u> (1987) and an Oscar for the screenplay for <u>Driving Miss Daisy</u>. His play <u>The Last Night of Ballyhoo</u> won the Tony Award for Best Play in 1996. In 1998 he won the Tony Award for Best Book of a Musical for his work on <u>Parade</u>. Uhry's musical <u>Love Musik</u> was produced on Broadway in 2008. He is the author of several screenplays including <u>Mystic Pizza</u>, <u>Rich In Love</u>, and <u>Tougaloo</u>.

Chapter Eight

Morning, New York City

HYLTON: You've had a quite diverse career in terms of having worked in film and stage quite extensively. Do you have a preference as to working in film or with theater?

UHRY: I feel lucky to have had my career in the movies. I like working with stage because in stage writers get the copyright. In films you don't get that kind of control. You don't get the copyright. Depending on who works on the project, you either get really lucky or unlucky.

HYLTON: How do you feel about directing your own work?

UHRY: I don't direct my own work. I never really wanted to do that. If I were a young guy starting out in film I might want to do that, like Kenny Lonergan. But I don't have a desire to do that now. It's important for me to have a good collaboration with the director, but to do it myself I think that's too many hats. I believe it's true that a director can take the role of an editor, like in film. There are plenty of writers who do good jobs editing their own stuff. Certainly David Mamet did good work directing his own plays. I think Edward Albee has directed some of his own work. I just don't think I could handle all of that. When a new play or musical of mine is being done for the first time, I am there all the time. I make myself available to all of the actors. I would never direct them, but for background questions or story help I am there. Sometimes I'll make a few changes in rehearsals. So I'm a pretty hands on writer and I'm pretty good at saying what I think to the director, but the older I get the less I would want to do that. But I do respect what a director does and I know the difference.

HYLTON: I understand you went to Brown and grew up down south.

UHRY: Grew up in Atlanta. I met a guy when I was at Brown. Brown had a musical comedy competition and a fraternity brother and I wrote a musical and got accepted. I think we actually wrote two. So he came from New York and he said, "Why don't we try and do this." So I came to New York and he's still my friend. He did the score for Driving Miss Daisy on stage. His name is Robert Walden. And we're talking about 1959 here.

I also got married right out of college. And it never occurred to me that I was going to have to make a living. And then we had a baby. It was dumb luck. In those days if you wanted to live with a girl, you had to get married. Before the pill, that's what you did. And that's what I did. And I'm still married. And I think I'm lucky in a way that my career did not get going early on. I had four children pretty quickly. So I spent a lot of time doing that. It's just the way it worked out for us. And my wife was working a lot. She was a teacher and still is. So I was putting things on the back burner unwittingly because I was spending a lot of time with my kids. But in retrospect, it couldn't have been better because I was there when they were little. And I wouldn't trade that time for anything. All of this really just fell into place the way it did. But I feel pretty fortunate that it happened the way it did. I got married, had kids and helped raise them, and then I found a career. I got to live through all of the parts. I'm glad it came out this way. My wife is a teacher at Fordham who teaches teachers how to diagnose learning disabilities. It's pretty esoteric and good focused work.

HYLTON: It sounds really interesting.

UHRY: I'm sure it is. But it's way out of my league. I mostly just do my writing out of my house, walk my dog, and she comes back. We have a place up in Dutchess County and live in the City part of the time as well.

HYLTON: I understand you have a Jewish background. Could you tell me more about your youth?

UHRY: I'm not sure how familiar you are with The Last Night of Ballyhoo, but that was basically my family. Jews with Christmas Trees. Easter egg hunts and all of that.

HYLTON: Must of have been interesting…

UHRY: I didn't know there was anything interesting about it at the time. I was pretty surprised when I got up here. I didn't know what a lox was and what a bagel was. And my wife is not Jewish. She's Episcopalian but she really has made me realize the import of having Seders and such. Really we behave like piss ass Unitarians. But we digress.

I wrote when I was a kid. I went to a county school in Atlanta and I was a total freak there. I liked to write, I liked theater, and I was straight. I didn't make any sense. But I was what I was. I was a crummy athlete. And so I was in my own box. I think I've always, sort of, been in my own box. So I went to Brown and I took theater. I met my wife. I knew that I wanted to do this. I came to New York and survived for a long time as a teacher at the Calhoun School, on the Upper West Side. I was teaching drama and some English Lit. And we survived on it.

HYLTON: Was the first film…

UHRY: The first film was <u>Mystic Pizza</u>. It wasn't my idea. They came to me. Sam Goldwyn was a producer and he knew I had four daughters. He said they wanted to do a female <u>Diner</u>. They weren't having a whole lot of luck with the scripts they were getting, so he put me on it. Frankly, the majority of the film stuff I've done has been rewrites and writing a lot of scripts that did not get made. And it's been great because it's supported me and my family for years. It was really my day job.

HYLTON: Did you ever do anything within television?

UHRY: No.

HYLTON: Glad about that?

UHRY: Well, not really. At the time that <u>Driving Miss Daisy</u> happened, I got offered to do a sitcom. I had no money for so long. And they were going to pay me fifty or sixty thousand a year. And that sounded great but I just had too much going on with Daisy at the time. And I'm pretty glad in the end I didn't do it then, because it wouldn't have been easy convincing my wife to move to L.A. I didn't want to live there.

I don't think that sitcom writing is really conducive to the type of writing I want, or like, to do. Because you sit in a room with thirty people and work together, and I'm glad to do the work myself. So, I don't think it's bad or good. I'm sure it pays well. I don't know many people who have gone and done for a long time television and come back and do plays. I know the other is true. I feel like I was lucky that I always loved movies and I had a natural ear for that stuff. And I always thought, "If you can write a play you can write a movie." But I don't think that's necessarily true. I think it just depends on what you hear and what you see.

HYLTON: Do you have a preference at this point?

UHRY: I would venture to say that for a real writer if theater paid as well as film, there wouldn't be many movies. You just have no control over the film. They own it. Once it's out of your hands it's out of them. I'm a theater boy. And I love both musicals and drama. I like the musical work because of the collaboration. It's far less solitary than writing a play for yourself. I get tired of myself.

HYLTON: So once you came to New York what happened?

UHRY: Well, we had to be pretty enterprising because we didn't know anybody. I was a Georgia boy. So my

114

friend said, "We're gonna go to Frank Lasser's office." Frank was a music publisher as well as a composer and lyricist. And Frank signed promising people to contracts. So he signed us and paid us fifty bucks a week and what it turned out to be was like a graduate seminar in writing. We would write stuff and take it up to Frank's office, every so often, and he would really critique it. And I learned everything I learned about how to write from Frank Lasser. He taught me to be clear, how to write lyrics.

HYLTON: So you were working on the book for the musical at that point?

UHRY: Actually, I was just doing the lyrics. I had already written the book in college. If you look it up, there's a musical in the annals of things called Here's Where I Belong. And that's when I had to go out and become a teacher. And I was lucky then too. I started to work at Goodspeed Opera and did about five things up there, but it was all about old shows and I was just redoing the book. I could experiment and do what I wanted, which was great because I learned a lot.

HYLTON: So you had an agent at this point?

UHRY: I always had an agent. Her name was Flora Roberts. Flora was Sondheim's only agent that he ever had. She was very interesting and colorful. I don't think agents really are there to get you work. She always said "I'm not an employment agency." And they're not. More in film and television do they serve such a role. I don't think agents can get you jobs. They can send your play around. After Flora died I didn't have one for a long time. But now I've signed up with William Morris. We'll see with them. So, for me <u>Driving Miss Daisy</u> happened and it happened big and ever since then I've been lucky enough to be doing all of this stuff.

HYLTON: How was it that you first got your agent?

UHRY: Bob Waldman's brother had friends who knew someone who was involved with Sondheim during his <u>West Side Story</u> days. So that person introduced us to Flora.

HYLTON: So what do you think is the angle a young playwright should take?

UHRY: I think the way to go is to focus on the work. And, frankly, having an agent didn't really change things for me. The work changed things. <u>Driving Miss Daisy</u> changed things for me.

HYLTON: And <u>Daisy</u> came through Playwrights Horizons. Can you tell me how that came about?

UHRY: Well, I wrote the play and my agent said "Where do you want it to go?" And I said I'd love it to go to Playwrights [Horizons]. This is back when Playwrights Horizons was up on the little theater on 42nd Street. I don't know if you were ever up there in the little theater or not but it had seventy-four seats. It was a great little black box. I saw a lot of stuff that I admired up there. Wendy's [Wasserstein] stuff, and many others. Playwrights back then was on top of a whorehouse. Actually, I guess it was more of a massage parlor. But there were prostitutes on the street. Back then 42nd Street was a funky street.

I didn't really know who Morgan Freeman was back then. I got him confused with a lot of other people. He just sort of said he'd like to do [my play]. And then I saw this movie called <u>Street Smarts</u>. He plays a pimp and I said, "Jesus, God. What have I got here?" And from the first rehearsal it was just right. Morgan and I are about the same age. We're both from the south. And he said to me "We must have known the same man down there." And that play was just a fire. Morgan was a miracle. And the fact that they gave him the role in the film was a tough road. They wanted Sidney Poitier, they wanted Danny Glover, and I was just lucky.

HYLTON: Did you have to fight for him at that point?

UHRY: I really couldn't fight for him. But people did ask me what I thought and I just said that I thought nobody could do the role like Morgan. And he and Dana are the two really close actor friends I have. A lot of the others are just hug, kiss, how are you, but those two are really my friends. He's the same guy he was back then. He flies around in his own airplane now but, he's the same guy. He deserves his success. He's a remarkable actor.

HYLTON: And how did <u>Driving Miss Daisy</u> become a film then?

UHRY: Well, it was a big hit. And Flora helped me shop it. She said, let's do Zanuck and Brown. She told me the movies they did, <u>Jaws</u> and <u>The Verdict</u>, and I was very lucky that they got Jessica Tandy and a great director. People wanted younger actresses but the director said it's not right to have some young girl tottering around there in makeup. So, they decided that Jessica was the only candidate and luckily she was well enough to do it.

HYLTON: So I see that recently you have chosen to work on musicals.

UHRY: I did <u>Parade</u>,which was a joy to make. It wasn't a great commercial success, but a joy. And it's now being done quite a bit in colleges. It was more fun than I ever had in my life. A pretty heavy duty, not fun thing to see, but a joy to do it.

HYLTON: At this point if you want to get something produced would you aim to go to regional theaters?

UHRY: Yes. Every time.

HYLTON: And why is that?

UHRY: I just think that New York is not for test market. Because once it's here, it's here. Having said this, if you trace the history of the musical, <u>Urinetown</u>, it was always in New York.

HYLTON: That started in the Fringe Festival.

UHRY: Yeah, way out there. But Broadway really isn't for plays much anymore. Usually you pretest it outside now.

HYLTON: So which are there theaters you gun for now?

UHRY: I would gun for someone I know. And luckily I know some people by now. But if I were a young playwright and I knew someone who was running the

"Shit-ass Theater" in "Nowhere" I would go there. Really, to someone you know…someone you trust. The other thing I have said to younger playwrights when I've spoken with them is "Work in theaters." Particularly not-for-profit theaters love to get free help. They are always looking for ushers. You get to meet the people. You see what's going on. Then you say, "Hey, guess what Joe. I wrote a play." And Joe knows you now so he says, "Oh, ok. Well I guess I can read it and there you go." I've seen that happen quite a bit. I think just picking up a handbook and sending out blindly is sort of the coward's way out. That's just sit and whine at yourself when nothing happens, instead of trying to do stuff. That's one thing that Daniel Goldfarb [writer of Modern Orthodox] did very successfully. And also he's good. He made contacts well. I would always advise people to work for not for profit theaters if given the opportunity. Why not? Nothing to lose.

DOUG WRIGHT

Doug Wright was born in Texas in 1962. After graduating from Yale University he earned his M.F.A. from New York University. He received the Charles MacArthur Fellowship, the Eugene O'Neill Theater Center Fellowship, and the Alfred Hodder Fellowship from Princeton University. Doug's play <u>Quills</u> won an Obie Award for Best Play. He later adapted the play into a screenplay which was produced, starring Geoffrey Rush. His work, <u>I Am My Own Wife</u> won the Pulitzer Prize and the Tony Award for Best Play. Wright wrote the book for the Broadway musical <u>Grey Gardens</u>, based on the Maysles brothers' documentary film. Doug currently has several screenplays in various stages of development in Hollywood.

Chapter Nine

Afternoon, New York City

WRIGHT: My parents took me to the theater when I was about nine in Dallas, Texas. And I think I was this sort of repressed, Presbyterian, gay kid who didn't feel a lot of license to express myself in the world. So at these little children's pantomimes I'd find that I was unleashing this emotional side to myself that I'd never been able to open up before. I became obsessed with the theater. And in Junior High I started a small little neighborhood theater group. My friends and I would mow lawns during the summer and save up to put on plays at the Town Hall.

I think I always wanted to create theatrical pieces. And in graduate school they forced me to check a box... Actor? Director? Writer? I was crippled by that because I thought to work in the theater you have to be expert in all three. How can you choose one? And it occurred to me, that to direct you needed a producer and a play and to act you needed a part. So for both of those crafts you required someone else's permission to practice them. And writing, all you needed was paper and some time.

And I thought, "That's control of your own destiny. You won't be reliant on other people to permit you to do what you love. You can just do it and follow it to where it leads you."

So I decided to go to graduate school for playwriting. And I went to NYU and got my masters there in 1987. And my thesis play was the first full-length play I'd ever written. And it was a play called Interrogating The Nude about Marcel Duchamp, the artist. And I submitted it to the O'Neill Playwright's conference and it was actually accepted.   I was so lucky because it was my school project and it was the first full length I'd done. So they were kind enough to workshop it there and it was subsequently performed at the Yale Repertory Theater. That was my first professional production of a full-length play.

In college I wrote and directed some productions and I acted in countless productions at Yale.   And in summers I carried many spears and lanterns in productions at the Berkshires, so I stayed very active. And in college I did an undergraduate major in theater studies and art history at Yale. But it was really the production at Yale Repertory, that made me feel like this was a plausible career for the future for me.

HYLTON: And you said that was written while you were in college or in graduate school?

WRIGHT: That was in graduate school within the NYU program. I did write a play while I was at Yale that we performed at the Yale Dramatic Association and that was subsequently produced at the Edinburgh Festival. [It was] a little one act play called The Stone Water Rapture, which I wrote when I was about nineteen. For better or worse it is still my most produced play. It's mostly [done] in secondary schools and training programs and colleges, but it is still the old warhorse. So that's how my educational theatrical career segued into a professional one.

HYLTON: So the one act you wrote in college was the piece that you submitted to get into NYU for the playwriting program?

WRIGHT: Yes, in fact, it was. So I submitted the one act to NYU and I was accepted there and there I wrote my first full-length play. Which is not entirely true. I wrote my first full-length play when I was eleven. It was this baroque gothic melodrama set in an English manor called The Devil's Playground, and everyone died in the end. And they all had names like Esmeralda and Ashton. And for my graduation from the New Dramatists last spring we did the first ever public reading of The Devil's Playground. When I wrote it, it was two hundred pages in longhand. And my remarkable, tolerant mother typed the entire thing because she knew that I wanted it to look like a real manuscript. So she typed it on carbon paper since we didn't have computers in those days.

HYLTON: Those were the papers that you could get high off of by sniffing them?

WRIGHT: Exactly, if the play didn't move you, then the carbon paper could. But actually the gesture of her giving that text enough credibility to actually pluck it out on a typewriter, all three acts of it, that was probably the first great gesture that gave me the confidence to pursue writing for theater.

HYLTON: And you acted yourself, directed, and wrote at Yale. How many plays do you recall writing while in college?

WRIGHT: I think I actually wrote four plays while I was at Yale. Two of which were actually performed and I directed. The other two were necessary abortions. They were plays that I was learning on, but I never inflicted on the unsuspecting public.

HYLTON: Do you keep copies of all of those?

WRIGHT: I think I do have copies of almost everything.

HYLTON: During that time were you taking classes in playwriting?

WRIGHT: I did take classes in playwriting. I took what they offered in the undergraduate level. And in those days you could audit courses in the graduate program. And I also would get bit parts in the graduate cabaret. And some of my older friends in the graduate program there would cast me in tiny supporting roles. So I felt like the Yale Drama School community was there for me but I went to NYU for my masters.

HYLTON: How do you feel that the NYU graduate program aided in your development?

WRIGHT: I guess it created the happy fiction that playwriting is important. Because it is such as a rarified form and the theater is so woefully under attended these days. And it's no longer part of our pop cultural life. It's become a sort of expensive hobby of an elite. And to say you are a playwright is like saying you're a gothic stone

124

carver, or a glassblower, or "I work in a Renaissance pleasure fair."

So by going to NYU for two years I put myself into an environment where people were as passionate about it as I was and still considered it a viable medium. So just that kind of unfettered enthusiasm and strength was fuel. And the program itself, like any program, was only as good as the professors that you sought out. But I was persistent and I got to work with Michael Weller and Terrance McNally, who was an extraordinary teacher. He was just a wonderful teacher. So getting to work with professional playwrights was especially gratifying because you weren't listening to stogy academics.

HYLTON: What kind of a learning environment did they create at NYU?

WRIGHT: With McNally we would bring in and read our works. Each student would read his or her plays aloud. He was extremely demanding. He would question your punctuation. But it was the kind of exactitude we really needed. He knew how to hold our feet to the fire. Weller was my thesis advisor. So he actually read my first draft of my thesis. And then he read through and gave me feedback on the second draft.

HYLTON: Did you develop a lot of relationships and make contacts through the program at NYU?

WRIGHT: In truth, no. There were certainly proactive teachers who would suggest potential routes for your work, but it's not like today I have a lot of interaction with my NYU peers. Curiously enough, when I was attending Yale, as an undergraduate, there was a very tight knit group of people who were seriously pursuing theater as a career and they ended up being many of the people with whom I work today. For instance, Jefferson Mays who acted in I Am My Own Wife is a college friend. He was at Yale. And Christopher Ashley, who directs much of Paul Rudnick's work, is a very dear friend. Tina Landau was there at the time as well. Several other actors were there as well in the Yale undergraduate school that are still working in theater. And I think we have helped one another at various times. Chris Ashley directed a number of my early plays when I was not getting produced and that was invaluable to me. Lisa Peterson read my work and helped facilitate readings on my behalf. I think the faculty at NYU was, in reality, more helpful in launching my work and the friends I made at Yale have become my collaborators now.

HYLTON: And by launching you mean precisely?

WRIGHT: I mean in the sense of suggesting avenues for my work or situations to develop my work in professional reading situations or possible one act festivals and ways of securing productions for my work.

HYLTON: Did you do the route that so many do, of taking the Dramatists' Sourcebook and papering theaters with plays?

WRIGHT: I certainly did. In graduate school I did it a bit with my one act. It didn't precipitate much but its appearance at the Edinburgh Fringe Festival did get it published. And that launched it. And that led to various productions while I was in graduate school.

HYLTON: And did Edinburgh come from a blind submission then?

WRIGHT: A friend actually saw it at the production at Yale. He was a young producer who was taking something to Edinburgh and he saw it and said he wanted to take it there. So he actually saw the college production if I remember correctly. I think part of it is, graduate school is useful because you get to know professors. And classes at places like The New School are useful because you get to meet more playwrights. I know I feel a sense of mission for young writers. I am incredibly gratified that this young playwright was working at New Dramatists as an intern. He slipped a note into my box and said he knew my work and asked if I'd be willing to read one of his full-length plays. And I said sure. And he wrote this gorgeous play. I passed it on to a friend at a theater in Philadelphia, at the Wilma Theater. She was intrigued and gave it a couple of readings and now it's slated for their season. And in a panel discussion the young playwright participated and amongst the people in the panel was Tom Stoppard. Because he is a wonderful and responsible human being, he read the playwright's work prior to the panel and was astonished by it and now Tom Stoppard is talking it up all over London. So things like that can happen. And the personal relationships you develop in school and outside can be more likely routes to eventual production than a blind submission from the Dramatists' Sourcebook. But, with that said, you never know.

And I would also say, you also can never be confident of the dividends of sending countless drafts to the theaters in the Dramatists' Sourcebook, because that gets your name circulated. If nothing else when someone says,

"Oh, John Doe, is a really compelling writer" and if a literary manager says, "I remember all of those manuscripts we got from John Doe" and if it gets another writer's sanction, it might actually get read. And so I'm not sure that I would say that such blind submissions are wholly frivolous.

HYLTON: What have you done in the way of self-producing material?

WRIGHT: I didn't produce my own work, but a group of Yale undergraduates led by Tina Landau started a Sunday afternoon salon because we were all sort of throwing ourselves into the pit of New York Theater production and we were all just trying to survive. And since we had a rich experience with one another as undergraduates we figured that maybe if we just had one day a week to check in with one another and maybe perform scenes or share work, it might keep hope alive. And so I did that and then I was actually asked to join a playwright collective at Playwrights Horizons. So I said an eager "Yes" to that offer.

There were no production opportunities, but I would sit in the basement of Playwrights Horizons on 42nd Street writing . Other members of the group were Peter Parnel, Peter Hedges, Aaron Sorkin, a wonderful actress named Connie Ray, and a cartoonist named Jeff Carey. We would bring in like five pages a week and I will never forget that Aaron brought in a couple of pages and he said, "I'm trying to write a screenplay and I couldn't do it. So, I've made it a play. And it's a military courtroom drama." So in the basement of Playwrights Horizons I originated the Tom Cruise role from A Few Good Men.

But being a member of those playwrights groups was great. We never knew if people were going to read our scripts or if they would ever get produced, but we did know that we had five pages on Sunday or Monday night that we had to read, come hell or high water, in front of people that we respected. And short of self-producing, I think staying active with other writers and holding myself up to a shared standard was really important to me. Otherwise I don't think I'd have had the fortitude to keep going.

Again, you're with a community of like-minded people who share a vision of the theater. That's really important and sustaining. Any kind of production, even if it itsn't a hit play is essential to your well being.

HYLTON: How do you feel about doing readings for your plays before production?

WRIGHT: I think there are two things here. I think first, as a writer, a reading is a necessary tool for assessing the state of your draft. And I know I find first readings of my work revelatory. Actors are suddenly applying their own thoughts and intuition to your work. An audience is trying to absorb it and follow it. And I have reams of notes after the initial reading of my work. And I require them in order to make the leap to the next draft. I couldn't bring my plays to completion without a series of readings. They often function, unfortunately, as tryouts for future productions of work. And that's fairly dispiriting because you can never fully control it. You can never control who is in the audience. And you can never really be sure that the play is ready to be exposed to that level of critique. And that's just a rather helpless circumstance. So I'm not really crazy about that. But a closed-door reading where I can assess what's working in the text is invaluable.

HYLTON: You've done a fair bit of directing. I wonder how you feel about directing as a writer?

WRIGHT: I think they can be inextricably linked. There's a very damaging bias against playwrights who direct their own work. And my smart-assed maxim is if Betty Crocker can write the recipe she can God damned bake the cake. And I really believe that. And oftentimes when you are sitting at your desk, if you are writing what is really a theatrically worthwhile piece, you are acting the roles. You are directing it as you craft a scene. And so often writers are treated as these idiot savants who just blurted out these pages of dialog and now require the help of seasoned veterans to shape it and craft it and coddle it into a play. And I just think that's incredibly condescending. And I think more writers should direct. More writers should act. I think they'd be better playwrights.

HYLTON: Would you apply your maxim to younger playwrights as well as the seasoned writers?

WRIGHT: Yeah. And fall on your face and make mistakes. And live too close to the work and learn what it means to take off one hat and don the other. And face the perils of it head on. Don't be precious about it and stand back and say "Somebody help me." Do it! And you may find you have a particular skill for it or you may not. If you're a good director and a good writer, chances are you can direct a good production of your play. If you're a bad director and a good writer, maybe you shouldn't. But I think there's room to do all of the above.

HYLTON: What makes up a good director in your mind then?

WRIGHT: I think it's someone who can tell you unerringly what you've written. Because I think there are always two plays in your mind. There's the play you think you've crafted and there's what actually is on the page. And a good director will use the actors, rehearsal hall, and everything he or she has to illustrate to you exactly what you have so far. And hold that in opposition to exactly what you think you have. And I think that's the best kind of writer/director relationships.

HYLTON: What were the bad relationships like then?

WRIGHT: It was those realtionships that lead me to start directing my own work. I've sat in so many rehearsals and listened to the director and said to myself, "Behave yourself. Sit quietly. You have to honor their process. They will get to it if you are patient. They'll get to it." And then about a week later the late night calls from the actors start coming. And they ask you, "What does [the director] want? Why are we not trying it this way? Did you see when I had an idea in rehearsal he quashed it?" And that's when you start directing from the backseat, which is unethical and inconvenient. So, there comes a point where you have to cut out the middleman.

HYLTON: Tell me more about your experience teaching at NYU.

WRIGHT: I was teaching an advanced playwriting course. Mark Dickerman, who runs the program at NYU was very generous and let me create my own course. And essentially I did a class on the One Act Play. I wanted every student to be able to bring a work to completion. And a one act seemed reasonable. So each student was required to draft a first and second draft of the play. And we would use their work as the raw material in the classroom. Because you could read one student's scene and the craft issues that they were confronting were illustrative for the entire class. So you could extrapolate many principles of good writing from specific works.

HYLTON: Did you use any textbook at all in addition to this method?

WRIGHT: This may make me sound like a school marm. But I think that every playwriting textbook in some way or another is usually predicated on Aristotle's Poetics. And he essentially said it all in that thin little volume about a character's journey and catharsis and the role of narrative in inducing a character's catharsis and unity of time and place and action. It's the most comprehensive volume on "How to create a story." So why read its gussied up versions when you can go back to the source? And so I use it a lot in the class.

HYLTON: In I Am My Own Wife the protagonist speaks about how you, as one of the main characters, had to sell personal items in order to support yourself. Was this a true statement?

WRIGHT: Yes, when I was working on I Am My Own Wife I sold my car in order to pay for another trip to Berlin. You know people seem to get a bit confused about the chronology of all of this. But I should go back to <u>Quills</u> for a moment because I think my experiences with <u>Quills</u> most accurately describe how I feel you really get ahead in this profession. So I'll come back to that in a second. But as far as the chronology, I had met Charlotte in 1992 and interviewed her in 1993 and 1994. I had all of these taped interviews and then proceeded to attempt the play and came up dry. And it was when I was trying to write <u>I Am My Own Wife</u> and feeling frustrated and abandoned it, that I decided to write a play about the Marquis De Sade. So I sold the car to visit Charlotte in late 1993 and I did not write <u>Quills</u> till 1995. So, my financial life did change rather substantially. And the thing about <u>Quills</u> is it taught me something so crucial. I was in New York. I'd worked in TV for a bit and tanked and was no good at it.

HYLTON: What were you doing in TV?

WRIGHT: I was working reading and developing for a wonderful producer, Norman Lear. But television wasn't my strength. And I came back to New York frustrated. I was living off of my TV savings. I ran out of money. All of a sudden I was thirty years old and calling for loans from my parents off of their retirement account. And I felt like the biggest loser in the world. It was heartbreaking. But I found this fellowship at Princeton University called the Hodder fellowship. And I was fortunate enough to get it. So I knew I had a year at Princeton when I would be fed, housed, have a stipend, and I could write without having to turn anything in. So I arrived at Princeton, grateful but deeply, deeply frustrated in my writing life. I was starting to think of a different career such as teaching in a university. And I thought "What the hell? If you're really going to abandon this, your last play should be the most reckless, audacious, nasty piece you could possibly concoct. And you should just write it to exorcise the demons. And fuck it if no one ever produces it." And so I started to write it, this fiendish little play called, <u>Quills</u>. And I would literally sit in my office on the second floor of the creative writing program at Princeton just cackling at my own obscene humor. And then I would turn all red and blush and put it away in the desk. I wrote it purely for myself and it really felt like opening a vein and just spilling it all over the page. And I had no urgency for it because I thought it was going to be my last work. So I didn't prescribe a future for it at all. And later a producer I know quoted Arthur Miller as once saying, "If there's something in the play that makes you ashamed, chances are it is a play you really need to write. And there's a good chance it will really be a good one."

And that's so telling to me because I wrote that play as a complete and utter expression of myself with no thought as to its future. Certainly no mainstream theater would ever want to produce it. So I put it in a drawer and said, "Well, you certainly let Pandora out of the box." And now chill out and come up with something that someone might produce. And it not only became my most popular play at the time but also my first, and only, big screen Hollywood feature. So I think it's really easy to distract yourself by chasing productions, writing cover letters to all of those theaters in the <u>Dramatists' Sourcebook,</u> or by asking fifty friends "How do you get an agent?" And those are all the ways that we as writers procrastinate from the very difficult, very challenging task of staring down the blank page. If you face down that page and if you really expose yourself in the bravest way, then people will notice.

I know that it almost sounds like some sort of weird alchemy, "How will they notice?" "When will they notice?" But it happens because, for all of our frustration, there is at the end of the day a dearth of really thrilling writing. There are so few times that you pick up a page and read and say, "Oh my God, that is a voice that I have never heard before." And when it happens, you never forget it. So I think Quills taught me that is the only way you can secure yourself a professional future. And that's by unleashing yourself on the blank page in an unfettered and completely honest way.

HYLTON: And many are afraid to do just that, be honest.

WRIGHT: Everyone is terrified to do that and everyone thinks they are writing for a market or to please literary managers or to please a subscriber audience or their parents, and you can't. And from the opening day of the production of Quills in 1995 at the New York Theater Workshop, I have earned a full time remunerative living as a writer. And so I think that is the leap you have to take. It may seem impractical but it is the only way. It is important to qualify all of that inspirational talk, since you ask what it was like from Quills to now, and the experience of turning Quills into a film demonstrated to the people in Hollywood that I had some screenwriting acumen. Since that time my day job is writing screenplays for Hollywood movies. So it would be misleading for me to say that I earn all of my living from writing for the stage. Even with a hit play on Broadway with a Tony and Pulitzer that income is not sufficient to pay the bills. And the royalties for the play have certainly picked up since the Tony, but even so, much of my life is paid for by screenwriting for Hollywood.

JOHN GUARE

John Guare was born in 1938 in New York City. He graduated from Georgetown University and the Yale School of Drama. Guare's play The House of Blue Leaves (1971) won an Obie Award and subsequently won a Tony for its 1986 Broadway revival. His play Six Degrees of Separation was nominated for the Pulitzer Prize and won the New York Drama Critics' Circle Award. Guare's produced screenplays include Taking Off (1970), Atlantic City (1980), and Six Degrees of Separation (1993). He is a member of the Dramatists Guild and was a playwright in residence at New York's Signature Theater.

Chapter Ten

Afternoon, New York City

GUARE: I knew I was going to be a playwright when I was eleven. I did three plays in 1949 in a garage across the street from where I still live. My parents gave me a typewriter for my 12th birthday, "To our playwright." And that was just it. I was going to be a playwright. I focused on seeing plays, watching them, and looking at them. And then when I got to Georgetown [University] they had a playwriting contest. And I wrote every year for that contest. I wrote my first musical with book, music, and lyrics by myself. Some of those songs ended up in House Of Blue Leaves. And then I applied to Yale and got in, against Georgetown's advice or help or aid.

HYLTON: What were they suggesting that you do upon graduation?

GUARE: Work in a bank. They just wanted all of their graduates to go into business so that you could be an alumnus and give them money. Georgetown was not challenging. They had very limited plans for their people. And then I went to Yale, and Yale was where my life began. And one of the great things was that in those days, it was the last gasp of plays going out of town to try out before they went to Broadway. Off-Broadway was something very marginal at the time. And so every week you'd see a new play. So plays got to be something that you would go and watch and say, "What would I do to fix this?" "What tools would I need to fix this?" I just read every play in the world that I could while I was at Yale. I took set design courses and lighting and costume design courses there. I became immersed in the theater. I got drafted when I got out. Luckily, I got into the Reserves. I came back to New York and in that time I was very lucky.

When I was at Yale, Audrey Wood, who was a legendary agent, saw my senior thesis play. She was Tennessee Williams' agent and she signed me as her client. Wow! Well, I was sort of overwhelmed by that and did not really know what it meant. Edward Albee, who is a hero of a lot of many American Playwrights' lives, took his money from Who's Afraid of Virginia Woolf and started the Barr-Wilder-Albee Workshop on Van Damn Street. The theater is still there. And for several years from 1963 to 1969 every ticket was free. It sort of ended with Boys In The Band and the emerging success of Off-Broadway. I became a member of Albee's theater and had a play done there.

Caffé Cino was just starting and that was thrilling. And there was all this activity going on. There were just all of these plays out there being produced that were not being covered by anybody. You'd just go to the Cino or La Mama to see what was on that night. And I remember that I heard Theater Genesis was having readings of new plays on Monday. I wrote a play on a Thursday and it opened up that next Monday.

Back in 1965 I had hitchhiked in Europe. During that time I wrote the first act of <u>House of Blue Leaves</u>. The Eugene O'Neill Theater Festival was starting in 1965 in Waterford, Connecticut. They picked the twenty names that were recommended by various Off-Broadway theaters. And I was on that list with Sam Shepard and Lanford Wilson. And we went up to Connecticut and the O'Neill People asked us what we would want in terms of support. A year later we came back and it was there. They had listened to us and [the O'Neill] became a real playwright's theater.

In 1966 we did act one of <u>House of Blue Leaves</u>. And from that I got a fellowship to go back to Yale for Brustein's first year as head of the Yale Drama School. We got five thousand dollars and a movie camera from ABC Television with the fellowship. So, Sam Shepard, Megan Terry, Ken Brown, Barbara Garson who wrote <u>MacBird</u>, and myself were fellows at Yale. It was a thrilling year. Robert Lowell was there, Irene Worth was there, Linda Lavin and Ron Leibman, and many other extraordinary artists were there. I had a thrilling time. I became great friends with Linda and Ron and I wrote a play for them. They met the first day [of the Festival] and got married. So it was like that.

The O'Neill Festival would give the writers a date for a performance. The writer would compose a play for that date. If you didn't have it, there would be a hole on that date, and you'd be embarrassed. It was wonderful. I wrote three plays: <u>House of Blue Leaves</u>, <u>Muzeeka</u>, and <u>Copout</u>. It was wonderful having that kind of trust. I realized after I did <u>Blue Leaves</u> that after that I would be judged by that play. But it was an extraordinary thing to be given that trust and to write for that.

Muzeeka was done in 1968 and Jerry Robbins had read the play and asked me if I would work at his American Theater Laboratory. He asked me to adapt a Brecht play. I did the Brecht adaptation. Leonard Bernstein and Stephen Sondheim came in on the production. 1968 was a nightmare year for me. But it changed my life. It was a horrible nightmare year since it was Bernstein and Sondheim's first work since West Side Story and both Lenny and Jerry became very fearful of the Brecht project. And Jerry, in particular, had an almost insane awe of Brecht that wouldn't allow any playing around with the material. The work collapsed on its own. Jerry walked away from it.

In 1986 the production came back to life. Jerry said "Let's go back to work on it." And it was quite different to come back to it eighteen years later. Lenny was quite tormented at that point and humbled by the events of his life between 1968 and 1986. He wanted a success and was terrified. He was wonderful and Jerry too. Steve was wonderful. Steve was eight years older than I but he was in the same position I was in with West Side Story. He was low man on the totem pole. Jerry was initially very Machiavellian in the first attempt. He was playing everyone off of each other. But the second attempt was wonderful. Steve helped guide me through and we all became very good friends through the 1986 experience. So, again thanks to those odd things of going to Yale, having the play seen by Audrey Wood, and then coming in at the right timing in 1964 when Off-Broadway was thrilling, it was a tremendously productive time.

My father once came to see a play I'd done at the Cino and he was horrified because at the end there were baskets handed around. I'd been supporting myself largely from that basket for ten years. My father was horrified that here I was, with a Yale Master's Degree, handing around a basket at the end of the performance. So he said, "I have an idea. Why don't you write a hit musical and then you can come back to the Cino." He didn't understand my life. I wrote House of Blue Leaves and it finally got on in 1971. From that Joseph Papp asked Mel Shapiro if he could do Two Gentleman Of Verona in [Central] Park on the truck. People were terrified of doing plays on the truck. Before they'd done the Scottish play, Macbeth and the cast was stoned. They had beer bottles and stones thrown at the cast. You know, "What did this have to do with our lives?" And people were worrying, "If they did that to the actors when they did Macbeth what are they going to do with this play with reflections on love?" So Joe asked me to come in and help shape the play into a ninety-minute form. And the composer would write some music for it.

We cast Raul Julia to lead a wonderful cast. And we wrote it in rehearsals. We went into rehearsals with six songs and came out with thirty more. It got delirious reviews and moved to Broadway. It won the Tony and had national tours, went to London, and had productions around the world. And suddenly I had this money and I was offered a lot of musicals. For instance David Merrick asked me to do a musical of Arsenic And Old Lace with music by Richard Rodgers for Ethel Merman and Mary Martin and I said, "Huh?" And I remembered what my father had said about "Write a hit musical and then go back to the Cino." So I left New York. I went up to Nantucket and started doing theater as a playwright. And my life changed then. I met my wife and started a new life. And then I started that lonely process of going anywhere where they would do your plays. Chicago was an incredibly valuable place for me. The Academy Festival Theater in Illinois had a dazzling history with productions like A Moon For The Misbegotten, with Jason Robards. It was a remarkable theater, just a fantastic theater. I was in Chicago when Steppenwolf was beginning. I had this play, The Landscape of the Body, that was done in Chicago and eventually came to the Public Theater in New York.

Sam Spiegel a very famous film producer, who did On The Waterfront, saw [my play] and bought it to do the movie. It was such a theatrical thing and I couldn't translate it. The play did not want to be a film. It was a naturalistic story about life in The Village. It couldn't be done as a film without the natural elements being lost. But also, about that time Louis Malle called me. My number was in the phone book. He asked me if I was the one who'd written that play that he'd seen the year before and if I'd had any ideas for a movie. He had the money for a film but no script. So Louis came to see me. I'd been fascinated by what was going on in Atlantic City at the time and that became the topic for our film together.

So everything seems so random but, when you look back, you can see how things connect. You mentioned that this is a book about how to get your work produced. The thing is, it is all about getting your work seen. It's very hard to control a career. All you can do is put your work out there and see what comes from it.

HYLTON: Did you ever have aspirations to direct the material yourself?

GUARE: I never wanted to be a director.

HYLTON: Edward Albee said when I interviewed him that he felt every artist had another artist within him. He wanted to be a composer and saw his language to be his version of musical pieces. Was there another form of art that you would have enjoyed working with?

GUARE: I enjoy drawing. When I was thirty-five I just stepped back and stayed out for a year. I took piano lessons and studied music theory seriously for a year. At the same time I was also taking trapeze lessons in Manhattan. It was a really unusual year. I did not know what the next step was going to be. If I was to continue playing music I knew I was going to have to put a lot more time into it. But it was a wonderful year, to be able, at age thirty-five, to immerse myself in something that had only been very tangential in my life before. Are there other types of artists inside the playwright? Sure. Tennessee was a great poet and he also drew. You cannot limit yourself. I don't think it's so amazing when you are interested in multiple forms of art. I think it's more unusual when a painter or a dancer or photographer only does that one art.

HYLTON: I understand you are still doing some teaching at this point?

GUARE: I still teach at Yale.

HYLTON: What are the changes you've seen in terms of the routes presenting themselves to playwrights today?

GUARE: Strangely, there are many more venues today. Many more theaters are eager to do a new play. The harder thing is getting a second production of a play. It's a completely different world now. But it's always very different. It's always changing. You have to always take the moment that is given to you. If you need to do so you have to start a new theater company to get your plays seen. You can't just sit back and say, "Oh, no one will read my plays." Because there are an enormous amount of companies and reading programs and steps you can take. You just want to get your work seen. That has always been the most important part.

As much as I can say it was helpful to be put up for the Albee Workshop or O'Neill, everything else I got was on my own. You can't sit and wait for everything to happen. I am a judge in several huge playwriting contests. The whole thing really is how you support yourself so your temporary job doesn't rule your life. But the situation always changes. By the time this book comes out the theater situation will be totally different. And that's what's thrilling about theater. But the one constant is, "How do I get my work seen?"

The good thing about going to the drama schools is that you can meet actors and directors with whom you can develop relationships. Drama school is now becoming prohibitive based on the expense of school. And that is the big change now. The expense of going to school is real. And forty years ago it was very cheap to live in the Village. It's impossible now. I couldn't afford to live in my apartment if I was just moving in. But I've lived here for thirty years. So the economic realities of life, and the inhospitality of life to a young artist, is the real change.

HYLTON: I understand from Katherine Graham's autobiography that you had some initial involvement with the New York Theater Workshop. What was your connection with NYTW?

GUARE: Jim Nicola, who was the director of the New York Theater Workshop, had been the casting director of the Public Theater. So we had become friends through the Public. However, Larry Arrick, a director, even to this day and even in the heyday of Joe Papp in the 1970s, only trusted a playwright if it came through a director who wanted to do the play. And I would say that still stands today. Larry had wanted to direct Bosoms And Neglect at the New York Theater Workshop which is how that happened. Years later, Jim Nicola gave Elizabeth Marvel a stack of plays. And she read my Lydie Breeze plays and she said, "I want to do these." And that's how that came about, with an actor wanting to do a play. It's very rare that a theater will have the vision to say, "Oh, I want to do this new play" unless it comes from an actor or director saying I really want to do this. The producers usually need an actor or director attached to crystallize its production before it will see a stage.

HYLTON: Would you tell me a little bit about your work in film over the years?

GUARE: In 1970, through the work I'd done at the O'Neill, I got to work with Milos Forman on his first American movie. It was called Taking Off. It is literally a lost movie. It won the prize at Cannes and was a wonderful movie. But for various reasons unknown, it has really never been seen and can't be found. I've written about six or seven screenplays and had three films made. Just a few years ago I withdrew from the Writers Guild. It's just too humiliating to work in the movies. The myth of movie money is just that, a myth. They pay you in so many steps that the big money is not received until the picture is made. And by that time they own you. You have no control over the film. You can be dropped at any moment. It's a humiliating experience. Now, a film director like Marty Scorsese or Stephen Frears, both of whom I worked with, had so many projects out there that my piece was just another arrow in their quiver, while for you, it is everything. And so it's just too humiliating to work in the movies. Strangely, the three experiences I've had, <u>Taking Off</u>, <u>Atlantic City</u>, and <u>Six Degrees of Separation</u>, were all wonderful experiences. But those were real anomalies. And you put as much work into that as you do into a play, and then nothing happens and they are not made. The writer is out of it.

HYLTON: How do you feel about the state of Broadway at this point?

GUARE: No one dreams about Broadway. Broadway is a marketplace. It used to be, when I was a kid, that you would dream about what was going to be your first play on Broadway. But now, I don't know of anyone who wants to put a play on Broadway. For instance, <u>Doubt</u>, it opens Off-Broadway and then makes the jump. No producer really aims to open a new play Off-Broadway any longer. It's just a marketplace.

HYLTON: What do you think it would take to "fix" the marketplace now?

GUARE: Federal funding. I've worked at a theater like the National in London. The range of work that they can produce is really exhilarating.

HYLTON: What would your final words be for a young aspiring playwright?

GUARE: There are a couple of things to keep in mind as a young writer. You yourself have to get your work out there. And the other thing is that tons of writers can write a perfect Harold Pinter play or David Mamet play. But the main thing is to find your own voice. What is most uniquely you? That is usually the hardest part for a person to recognize about himself.

STEPHEN ADLY GUIRGIS

Stephen Adly Guirgis was born on New York City's Upper West Side. He was nominated for a Drama Desk Award for his play Our Lady of 121st Street and an Oliver Award for Jesus Hopped The A Train. In 2005 Time and Entertainment Weekly Magazines both listed his play The Last Days of Judas Iscariot amongst their Ten Best Plays of the Year. He is a member of New York's LAByrinth Theater Company and the New Dramatists. Stephen has also written for television shows including NYPD Blue and The Sopranos and created the show, The Get Down with Baz Luhrmann.

Chapter Eleven

Afternoon, New York City

HYLTON: I understand you graduated from SUNY Albany with a degree in drama. What did the degree do for you?

GUIRGIS: Nothing. But [SUNY Albany] is where I met John Ortiz and several other people I work with today. If I hadn't gone there I wouldn't have met John or gotten involved in the LAByrinth [Theater Company]. If I hadn't fucked up and stayed in school so long I would have graduated before he got there and been out of there. So I guess it worked out.

After college I helped start a theater up in the Bronx called "The Belmont Playhouse." I did that for a few years. I did that with two other actors, Marco Greco and Dante Albertie. We literally built the theater. It was around for eight or ten years. But I didn't want to run a theater.

Then I fucked around in New York for a few years. I went to acting school at the William Esper Studio. I went to acting class, studied Meisner, went to the LAByrinth Sessions, and went to therapy. And after that, my life really started up. I guess the way things happened for me was sort of, unintentionally. I started writing things for the LAByrinth. They encouraged us to write our own stuff and do different things. And for the first couple of years, we weren't producing anything or really intending to stage anything. It was really just a collective, a gym for actors. When we started to produce, we decided to do everything in-house. Eventually John asked me to do something. I wrote a little one act. And it went well. From there the company just kept encouraging me to keep writing. So I didn't really intend to become a writer. I didn't really intend to have an agent as a writer. But eventually, it just sort of came about.

I've had a fortunate experience. I have never written a play that hasn't been produced. Everything I've written has gotten done. I've been very fortunate.

But also, I guess, the only thing that separated me from being a writer and not being a writer, aside from the fact that I joined a company that pushed me to be a writer, was actually sitting down and writing. Because it is just as easy to not sit down than to sit down. For a long time I regretted my twenties where I wasn't that productive. Then again, I think I stored up a lot of experiences that I guess I could write from. It is difficult to let go of regrets. But everything that happens to us gets us to where we are and where we are going tomorrow.

HYLTON: How did you support yourself while you wrote?

GUIRGIS: I worked in restaurants actually from seventh grade up till Jesus Hopped The A Train got produced. I bused tables, waited, and bartended. My next job was my work in arts education. I helped educate people about drugs, STDs, and violence prevention in schools and prisons. It was important work for me because it was the first time that I got to use what I was trained for in college to do something positive for people. I was able to help combat issues in a way that I couldn't by serving someone a cheeseburger or a martini.

I got into the arts education through some people in the LAByrinth Theater Company, who were involved with the program. We were working all over the boroughs, in Brooklyn, Bronx, and Manhattan. It was really rewarding. I would love to get back into it. It was a good thing. I did that for about four or five years.

It got to a point when I had to stop doing it when I couldn't write and work at the same time. I remember I was really broke. But it was time to take a chance and make a commitment. I couldn't work full time and write. I felt like I had to take a chance at writing a play. So I let go of the work and dedicated myself to the writing.

I wrote In Arabia, We'd All Be Kings in 1999. We used to read new works once a month at the LAByrinth. We had this girl who was supposed to write something for us and then, a few days before we were supposed to do her work, she bailed out. We already paid for the theater so I sat down and wrote for four days and that ended up being the first chunk of Arabia. It was about the first fifty pages. So we read it, and then after the reading John and Phil [Seymour Hoffman] said, "Let's do this play." And I was like, "Well, I just started writing it." They asked me who I wanted to have direct it. I said, "Well, how about you Phil?" And he said, "I haven't directed before." And I responded, "Well up until about a year ago I never wrote before." Phil acted in a play I wrote earlier and that's where we met and discovered that we had a similar sensibility about what goes on, on the stage. So he said, "Ok, I'll direct it." So we rehearsed it and put it up.

That was the first show where [the LAByrinth] paid for a publicist. We were at a place as a company where we either had to get people to see us or agree to be a place where people would just hang out. We put our energy forward to making a good show and letting people come see it. I think that was the play that started to put us on the map.

HYLTON: So since you already had a home with LAByrinth it sounds like you were able to skip the blind submission process?

GUIRGIS: Yeah, I was just out at a playwrights' conference and people were talking about [sending out their plays]. And it happened a little bit to me. I mean once I got an agent they sent out my plays and some people didn't want to put them on stage. But I always had my place where I wanted to do my plays. The good thing about having a home is that the actors know each other. Everyone, therefore, works harder. I know I'm really lucky.

HYLTON: How did you end up getting your agent?

GUIRGIS: I ended up with my agent, John Buzzetti, during In Arabia. I met him a few yeas before when he was an assistant. I wasn't into being a writer. So when someone gave me their card I wouldn't call them. Then when In Arabia came out lots of people started calling me. I remembered John from before and I liked him a lot. He seemed like he really believed in my work. So that was that.

Once you get an agent they are going to push you in the direction of stuff that makes money. They kept asking me to do TV. My way of deflecting it was I said, "I only want to work with David Milch or Tom Fontana." To me there was nothing else interesting on TV. And the next day I started working with this manager, through my agent. I told the manager my stance and the next day I was sitting down for breakfast with David Milch and he offered me a job. So I had no choice.

As you know it's really difficult to make a living as a playwright. I think the pay for <u>Jesus Hopped The A Train</u> and <u>In Arabia, We'd All Be Kings</u> were like $250 for the whole thing. So David Milch had a show in New York. I got to stay in New York and make money and get health insurance and everything. The show was called <u>Big Apple</u>, and although it didn't last that long, it was a good experience. Then they wanted me to go out to L.A. for meetings and stuff. I went to L.A. and I got an offer to do another NBC show. At the time I was assisting John Patrick Shanley on a play. I asked if I could help him because I've always loved him as a writer. And then I got this offer to go to LA and work on this big network series. I didn't know what to do. Then when I thought about it, I realized I was afraid to go and do the TV show. So I decided I should do the show. Plus, Shanley encouraged me to take the job.

The show was a great experience. Before I got that job I didn't know how to use email. I just knew how to write. I happened to land on a show where the boss really liked my writing. So I started as a staff writer, but I was writing from the beginning, got some money, and was able to give some money to my parents. Then 9/11 happened, and I was in L.A. I was in the office because I worked a lot. I basically slept in the office most of the week. I was writing something for them and then the security guards came in and called me over to the TV. I saw what was happening.

Then my boss called, because the episode we were working on talked about terrorism, and he said we couldn't do the episode. So he called and said, "I need you to stay at the office and write another episode. " And I asked, "Write another episode about what?" And he said, "About anything. But we need it in two and a half days." It was crazy because I was the only one from the office who actually lived in New York. The studio lot was closed for security reasons and I was locked in there writing a series show while watching the city that I grew up in burn down. I remember very distinctly thinking to myself, "The first chance I get, I have to get out of here and go back to New York. I'm going home."

I've always felt like whatever talent that I have for writing I didn't do anything to get it. I always think, "Who knows how long it will last." I remember at that time thinking, "I need to go back to New York and write about things that are important to me and mean something to me."

So the show got canceled at that point. I did some episodes of The Sopranos freelance and I did some NYPD Blue freelance. [NYPD Blue] actually was a really great experience. That office of writers was great and organized and a fantastic experience for me. I came back to New York. But before I moved back, I had meetings for other projects and I got offered a job on another show, which was actually a good show, and they were offering me a lot of money. It was more money than I thought I'd ever make. So I had a bit of a decision to make.

I thought about it and I realized I was afraid to not take the job. So, for that reason I didn't take the job. I kept thinking to myself, "I'll never get another offer like this again. I'm going to be forced to wait tables again." And then I realized my fear and I was like, "Fuck it. Time to go back to New York." It was a good decision on my part. I wrote Our Lady of 121st Street. I wrote Judas. I acted in a couple of movies. TV writing can be great and can be great money, but it's essentially ten months a year and they own you. I'm glad it worked out how it did.

But from the same token, you have to make money. And I am not in any way against the idea of television. People watch TV. That's not going to change and no matter what you're working on there is always going to be a good example of that genre. And as long as you're working hard on what you're working on, and trying to do good work, I think that is respectable. I grew up watching TV. I don't have a TV because I would watch it all the time. I learned about story from TV. It was helpful. There are some smart people out there making billions of dollars mixed in with the idiots.

HYLTON: I know you still work with the LAByrinth Theater Company. How does the LAByrinth find scripts for productions?

GUIRGIS: We now solicit scripts for the summer intensive. Overall, people can go through agents or through friends when they want to submit to the LAByrinth. I'd say LAByrinth members or friends write fifty percent of the scripts we do. Twenty-five percent come from agents and probably another twenty five percent come from people we meet or like. The strong emphasis is doing work written by LAB members.

I try to help the young playwrights at the LAB with their process. If they want someone to read through their rewrites, I try to help out. I have referred people to agents. We have to have good playwrights.

CHARLES SMITH

Charles Smith was born on the South Side of Chicago. He is a member of the Playwrights Ensemble at the Chicago Victory Gardens Theater and the New Dramatists. In 2008 he received the Ohio Arts Council Individual Excellence Award. His play <u>Black Star Line</u> was nominated for the Pulitzer Prize. Smith has had plays produced Off-Broadway and regionally and he is the recipient of multiple commissions from theaters including the Goodman, Victory Gardens, and Seattle Rep. He is currently the head of the professional playwriting program at Ohio University.

Chapter Twelve

Afternoon, Ohio

HYLTON: How did you become interested in theater?

SMITH: For me it was relatively late in my life. As a kid growing up in Chicago, I had never seen a play before. I dropped out of high school halfway through my freshman year. The Chicago Public School System and I determined it would be best if we parted ways. I hated school, I was fifteen, and the Vietnam War was going on. At that time all you had to do was go to the Draft Board and say "I'm eighteen" and they would register you for the draft. And they asked you for absolutely nothing [to prove your age]. So I used my draft card to get a driver's license, I used [the driver's license] to go to Chicago Heights and get a job. I was hired to work at one of the steel mills where I stayed for several years. The old guys working at the mill talked me out of staying at the factory, because I could read. I was one of the only guys working there who could read. Around that time my Uncle, who lived in Kansas, died. When I went to the funeral his wife was really upset and didn't know what she was going to do. And I had this calling and thought to myself, "This is it. I'll move to Kansas." So I left the mill and moved to Kansas.

When I got there I was eighteen or nineteen, but everyone thought I was twenty-two or twenty-three. I figured I'd get to Kansas, get a real driver's license, and start telling people how old I really was. I thought it was my opportunity to start a new life. When I got there, a lot of things happened in very quick succession. I met a woman who was a lot older than I was. We moved in together. We got married , and within a year we were divorced. I immediately went back to Chicago and was reunited with my childhood sweetheart who had gotten married after she heard I had gotten married. She found out I was divorced and decided that she too was going to get a divorce. What she didn't plan on was her hot-tempered husband's response. He murdered her on the spot. This was less than a month after my divorce. So I walked into the draft board and asked them to get me out of there. I said to them, "I want someplace far, what do you have?" They said "How about Korea?" So I went to Korea for a year and later, went on exercises to Germany. While in the army, I got my G.E.D., and got into photography. My Uncle was a painter who taught me about composition and I was always drawn to visual expression.

While in the army I found and read a copy of the The Illiad. It blew me away and reminded me of a book I read in school that had actually been banned by my grade school. It was Claude Brown's Manchild In The Promised Land, the reading of which was perhaps the highpoint of my time in the Chicago Public School System. While the two worlds of Manchild and Illiad are vastly different, the journey of both main characters is very similar. After reading The Illiad, I wanted to read more stories like that. And those two books made me want to write about, and explore, my own journey. I started taking college courses while in the army, mostly in English, studying the works of Homer, Chaucer, and Milton. When I got out of the army I wanted to take more classes, so I ended up in a community college in Chicago. They didn't have any English courses I hadn't already taken so I registered for a theater course and ended up acting in the first play I ever saw. I had a couple of lines and nobody could understand what I was saying. But it was fascinating being backstage. It was storytelling being done by a community of people and I was really attracted to the idea of a community of artists telling a story. So while sitting backstage during the run of the play I started writing my own plays. I showed [my plays] to a Professor and he said, "You shouldn't be here. You should be at the University of Iowa in their writers workshop."

The Professor had graduated from the University of Iowa and so he literally put me in the car and drove me there. I didn't know anything about Iowa. I didn't even know it was the next state over. So we went there with my stack of scripts. The guy running the program was a Scottish playwright named Tom McGrath. I walked in and handed him a bunch of scripts and said that I wanted to be in the Playwrights' Workshop. Tom read them and called me back and said "You're in." Meanwhile, what I didn't know was, it was a graduate program. And the University said, "You have to declare a major." And I didn't want that. Based on my experience with the Chicago public school system, I knew didn't want to go back to school. I just wanted to be in the program to write plays. But they said, with the courses I had already taken, if I took two additional English courses I could get an English degree. But when the other writers in the program found out I was an undergraduate, in the graduate program, they wanted to throw me out. But Tom said, "Let him stay." So I stayed and completed my undergraduate degree and an MFA.

When I was in school at Iowa, I had been self-sufficient for a number of years. I attended school under the G.I. bill, however, the University told me I had to supply my parents' financial information. I found this to be really insulting. I hadn't lived with my mother and brothers and sisters for years and was very proud of my independence. In retrospect, I think I was also a little embarrassed by the fact that my mother had no income. Finally the university said, "There's nothing we can do for you until you give us your parents' income information." So I said, "My mother has no income. There, are you happy?" And they said, "Ok, now look at additional financial aid you're eligible for."

The strangest thing for me was the first holiday at school. I'd ask my friends, "What are you doing for Christmas?" And they'd say, "I'm going home." And I said, "Oh, I'm going to be at home too." It wasn't until the holiday hit and I started calling friends, that I realized that when they said they were going to be at home, they didn't mean at home on campus. For me the only home I had was there on campus.

But the program was interesting. There was no structure to it so everything we learned, we learned by trial and error. The rest of the department just left us (the writers) alone. We had our own theater and when we got ready to do a play, the only people we had to clear it with were each other, the other writers, to make sure there were not scheduling conflicts. There was no one there to say, "This is how you do it." As a consequence, everything I learned about structure in storytelling, I learned since I left the program. There were classes, and a Playwrights' Workshop where we had our plays read and gave each other feedback, but there was not one course where they said, "This is how you tell a story" or "These are traditional storytelling features" or "This is what the audience is looking for." There were plenty of people to tell you what you did wrong after you wrote it, but no one to tell you how to approach the idea in the beginning. I think if I had learned some of those things I would have gotten a quicker start on my career and it would have saved me a lot of time. If I stumbled on something that was working in terms of structure back then, it was pure luck. But the amount of work we had to do, the amount of "butt in the seat" time that you spent writing to stumble upon a structure . . . well, I can say if writers do jump off a bridge, I know the reason why. It's much easier if you're provided with a bag of tricks that you can use so you can move on and do what you have to do.

We'd get students from the acting program to do our plays. There were probably between nine and twelve playwrights in the program. I started at Iowa 1979 and left in 1984 and then the University gave me an offer to stay and teach. I stayed one year to teach and after that year, they made an offer for me to stay longer. But I knew then I had to leave if I wanted to be a playwright. I loved being on a college campus. Growing up the way I did, a college campus was an oasis for me. But I knew I had to leave.

I faithfully subscribed to the <u>Dramatists Sourcebook</u> and tried to target specific plays to specific theaters while in graduate school. I figured I'd send off my play and they'd call me the following week. And when they didn't call within a week, I became indignant. Finally, I realized that I was not the only playwright out there and everyone else was sending out their bad plays as well. I had one play that I sent to PlayLabs, which at the time was run by Dale Wasserman and had an impressive reputation. They chose my play, along with six or seven others, for their summer workshop. I was assigned a dramaturge, the plays were read, and we all received notes. After rewriting over the summer, we reconvened and went into rehearsals that culminated in staged readings. Not only did I learn a lot about story telling over that summer, but I met a lot of good people. I worked with actors like Stephen McKinley Henderson, directors like Bob Falls, and dramaturges like Jonathan Abarbanel. I've kept in contact with many of the people I met that summer and have been very fortunate to have had the opportunity to work with a lot of them again.

I also did an internship at the Mark Taper Forum. A few years later, the former Literary Manager from the Taper, Russell Vandenbroucke, was working as Associate Producer of the Repertory Theatre of St. Louis. He sent me an brochure for three plays they were doing through The Imaginary Theatre Company, which was the Rep's outreach program. The third play titled <u>Tales of South Africa</u> was a play about modern day Africa using traditional song and folktelling. In the letter that accompanied the brochure, Russell asked if I could write the play described in the brochure. He could pay $750 for the play. I said, "Sure, I can write that play." I sat down and wrote the play within a few weeks. Then, I didn't hear from them for what seemed like ages. Eventually I heard back from Tony Kushner, who was also working with the Rep and writing for The Imaginary Theatere Company as well. Tony called to say that they wanted to produce the play. That was my first production after PlayLabs.

I also did an internship at the Victory Gardens Theater, reading scripts, signing rejection letters, and getting coffee. I did that without pay for about six months. When I started running low on funds, I considered looking for real work when the theater announced that they could start paying me. It wasn't a lot, but it was enough for me to continue working at the theater. Eventually, they brought me on as a full time salaried Literary Manager. All the while I kept on writing. Reading scripts and working as Literary Manager helped me quickly recognize some common mistakes playwrights make. It also gave me a perspective of how my work ranked on a national scale. In addition, when I had some material I needed to hear, I could easily set up a reading at the theater. Early on, when the Artistic Director, Dennis Zacek, found out I was a writer, he asked to see some work. I gave him a play of mine called Jelly Belly. He said he liked it a lot but couldn't produce it because he thought the raw language would turn off the subscribers.

Everyday, over a period of six months, Dennis would come into the office and tell me how much he liked the play, but quickly remind me that he couldn't produce it. Finally, one day he came in and told me how much he liked the play and, to hell with it, he was going to produce it. Eventually, Victory Gardens ended up producing the play three times: first in the VG studio, once in New York with Woodie King Jr., and once as a revival on the VG Mainstage. Most of my career as a writer has been in Chicago, because of Victory Gardens. It never occurred to me to move to New York. I figured I'd stay in Chicago because they were producing plays in Chicago. I now live in Ohio where I teach at Ohio University, but I remain a member of the Victory Gardens Playwrights Ensemble.

There was another writer in Chicago, Arthur Morey, who was teaching at Northwestern University. And he said, "Why don't you come out to Northwestern and teach classes?" And my response always was, "No, I hate that stuff." After repeated requests, I finally went out and taught a playwriting course and the University thought it went over great. They offered me an opportunity to teach full time. And I turned it down. When they asked why, I said, "You're not gonna like what I want to teach." They became curious and asked, "What're you going to teach?" I said, "I'm going to teach them everything you've taught them are lies." And they said, "That's great."

We later had this long meeting where I explained to them all of the reasons why I couldn't take the teaching job. I told them I wasn't interested in driving out to Evanston three or four times a week. And they said, "You don't have to. We can give you everything you want." I didn't realize we were in negotiations. I thought I was simply explaining to them why I couldn't take the job. I also didn't realize how much money they were offering. When I found out, I went back to the theater and I said, "Sorry, guys, but I have to go." So I started by doing a one-year contract at Northwestern. After I started, I didn't cash the first couple of checks. I wasn't used to making that much money and I thought the amount of money was a mistake. I figured they were going to eventually come looking for me to pay the money back.

After teaching there for a couple of years, I thought, "The money is good, but I'm earning every bit of it." After working there for a couple more years, I thought, "Time for me to get a raise." The money was great in the beginning, but I had increased my standard of living. And when my wife and I had a baby, I realized that the money that was once a luxury in my life, had now become an absolute necessity. And I was still working on one-year renewable contracts. About the same time, Arthur Morey, who got me the job in the first place and who was also on a series of one-year renewable contracts, didn't get his contract renewed and found himself out of work. That was a wake-up call. So I ended up leaving Northwestern and taking the job I have now at Ohio University. I took the position believing that I would be here for three years and then go back to [Chicago]. But we stayed. The University in Ohio has made my life easier and I have become a better writer for it.

HYLTON: I heard you are a member of New Dramatists. Can you tell me about your experience with them?

SMITH: New Dramatists was great. I absolutely loved coming to New York and staying there on 44th and Ninth. It really changed the way I was able to live and work while in New York. Being a member of New Dramatists removed a lot of that basic survival pressure. Now that my seven years at New Dramatists are up, the University gives me an expense account that helps with travel, room and board for my trips to New York, but it doesn't compare to the resources supplied by New Dramatists. As a member of New Dramatists, I not only had a place to stay and work, but if I needed to hear some of my work, they'd set up the reading, they'd help cast it, and would give you the space for the reading. Perhaps the richest resource supplied by New Dramatists is the first floor reading room. You'd sit in that room and you'd never know who'd walk in the door. And no matter who did walk in, you'd know that you all shared a common goal. It was a very rich time in my life.

HYLTON: I know you've written several pieces that are biographical studies of historical figures. What's motivated this decision?

SMITH: I wrote a play a few years ago on Marcus Garvey and I realized the theater responded very favorably because it had a built in P.R. Line. I realized that although people at the time didn't know me from Adam, the theater could say "Marcus Garvey" and people would pay attention. So I realized, "Wow if you have a hook like that you may be more likely to get produced." So I did a series of those types of plays, plays with what I thought were built-in PR lines. All of them were produced and while I'm very appreciative, I now find myself trying to escape from that historical playwright pigeon-hole.

HYLTON: What do you tell young playwrights when you give them advice on how to approach a career in playwriting?

SMITH: I think the biggest struggle is finding your voice and being true to that. When I was in graduate school, I remember being pretty surly and contacting the Goodman to find out why they hadn't produced my play. Greg Mosher, who was the artistic director at the time, wrote me back and said he'd be happy to talk to me if I were ever in Chicago. So I called and said I'd be in

Chicago in a few days and we set up a meeting. Greg was very kind to me and extremely generous with his time. I arrived in Chicago, they gave me a tour of the facilities, and I ended up in a room with Greg and six or seven other people, including Steve Scott who's still there. Greg began by asking if I had any questions and I went straight for the jugular. I asked why they weren't producing my play. Greg responded by saying, "Next season, we're doing a Tennessee Williams play, a new David Mamet play, and a new John Guare play." Then he looked me straight in the eye and asked, "Why should we do a Charles Smith play?" I stuttered, stammered and didn't know how to answer. Greg thanked me, we all shook hands, and they escorted me to the door.

But I thought about that meeting for a very long time and today, I know the answer to that question. The answer is that while all of these other writers may be good writers, none of them can write a Charles Smith play and a Charles Smith play is unlike any of these other plays. Finding your voice means understanding that you are not in competition with any other writer, because any writer who has found his or her voice is truly unique. This is the one thing I think writers who are young in their development have the hardest time understanding. You are not in competition with any other writer in this country. And you don't have to go out searching for your audience. Once you find your voice and your voice becomes clear, your audience will find you.

ROMULUS LINNEY

Romulous Linney was born in 1930 in Philadelphia, but spent his childhood in the South. He is a novelist and playwright who has had plays produced internationally. Linney has received Guggenheim, Rockefeller, and NEA fellowships and has won Obie and National Critic awards. He has taught playwriting at Columbia University, Princeton, and the University of North Carolina, Chapel Hill.

Chapter Thirteen

Afternoon, New York City

LINNEY: I grew up in North Carolina. For five years we lived in Boone, NC in the Appalachian Mountains. And we moved to Tennessee, but we went back there because my family was very much attached to that area. My father was a doctor. He died when I was thirteen. My mother and I moved from Tennessee to Washington, DC. During the war we were on 16th Street and then we got an apartment on Connecticut Avenue. My mother remarried a wonderful man and we lived in the Westchester Apartments.

I was motivated to act when I saw a production of <u>Our Town</u>. My mother was acting in it, playing Mrs. Gibbs, and I went to see it. I thought I'd be bored, so I brought chocolate cupcakes to eat. But I was utterly riveted by it. And I saw my mother on stage and I thought, "Wait a minute. That's my mother, not yours." I started crying and was very moved by the play, as I am sure you were too. It's a great, great play. That planted the seed.

I went to Oberlin College and I immediately started acting. I thought the world of it and thought I never wanted to be anything else but an actor. I went and did summer stock a lot and then went to Yale Drama School for a year. I got drafted into the Army. And when I got drafted something started to change. I spent two years doing garrison duty at Schofield Barracks in Hawaii. And things began to change. When I came back, I changed my major to directing. But there was something still wrong. I came into New York and went through the rather painful process of becoming a writer. The first thing I did was write novels. I had a job as a stage manager with the Actors Studio, that kept me involved with the theater. But I never thought about being a playwright. I thought I was going to write novels. I wrote two novels. I got published and everything was going all right. And then for the third book, I wrote a play. And that got produced at the Mark Taper Forum in its first season and it was successful. I then became a playwright and since then published another novel and many plays and some short stories.

HYLTON: How did you support yourself once you moved to New York?

LINNEY: I made fifty dollars per week at the Actors Studio. And in 1958 that wasn't so bad. I lived very simply and I did fine. I was living on the Upper West side sharing an apartment with another person. Then I went down and taught at the University of North Carolina for a while. Then I came back when I got a job teaching at the Manhattan School of Music, when it was over on the East Side. So the rest of my life was devoted to teaching and writing. And the teaching that I did there was at a time when I had to get a younger daughter through college. It was all adjunct teaching at that time. You didn't make any real money, but you were not part of an academic rat race either. So for forty years of my life that's what I did, teach and write.

HYLTON: I understand you were teaching at Columbia for some time. What was the experience like teaching there?

LINNEY: There wasn't any real process at Columbia at the time I was teaching there. It came to have some. Eventually it changed to a department about conceptual theater, which was fine. I then got a job teaching at the Actor's Studio program at the New School. And because of my experience working with the Actor's Studio, which as I mentioned was as a stage manager and then in the New Director's unit, I had a very good time helping to structure that program. And I was there for six or seven years before I retired. I had really a great time teaching there and I liked that program very much.

HYLTON: What are your classes like?

LINNEY: Well, the way I teach is I have them read their plays and then we talk about them. It's very simple. Columbia was a funny school. The arts at that time were not really well supported. The students who came there at that time thought, "Well, I'm in this great Ivy League school, but the school was not really generous to the artists. The playwrights had to do their plays in the basement of this old building.

HYLTON: Was this before the Arthur Miller Theater was there?

LINNEY: Well, the Arthur Miller Theater is not actually well geared for plays. There was a good place for plays, but then they redid it and it now feels a lot like a concert hall. But that's the theater that's been there for a while. Regardless, Columbia was very good to me. I made very good money working with them. I had an offer to go to Duke and Columbia matched it so I could stay. And I got my younger daughter through college that way and it was fine. I paid her graduate school tuition that way. And so I am very thankful to Columbia for that. But I must say that I was not at ease in that program. I had some very fine students, but I had many that had one foot in and one foot out. Whereas, at the New School they were very much into writing. They wanted to do it. They threw themselves wholeheartedly into writing plays in a way that I was very pleased about.

HYLTON: Are you still teaching?

LINNEY: I still go down to the Sewanee Writer's Conference. And I do a thing for the Ensemble Studio Theater up here in New York.

HYLTON: How did you get involved with Ensemble Studio Theater (EST)?

LINNEY: Well, I've had many plays done by EST. The playwright Michael Weller took me to EST when it was just two or three years old. And I liked it and got pretty involved with it. I became pretty good friends with Curt Dempster. And over the years I've done several plays with them. It is a very good theater.

HYLTON: How did you get your first play produced at the Mark Taper?

LINNEY: My play was the second play at the Taper. It was brand new. They opened with The Devils by John Whiting and mine was the second play. And it was very successful there. I did not get along with the director, unfortunately. So the play didn't make it to New York till later. There were two productions later in New York and then in Jersey and eventually all over the place afterward. It was produced in Europe in Vienna and did very well. The main thing about having that production was, it was a very daring and bold drama about Frederick the Great. It was not what you'd expect someone to write. And it was too long. And there were things I did not know about writing plays. And there was some conflict. But the fact that I had published two novels, and that they had been very well reviewed, helped. I wasn't just a playwright. And indeed, the publisher, Harcourt Brace, said they would publish it as a play no matter what happened. So I was fortunate that I was able to withstand much of the tough stuff.

HYLTON: Did you have an agent at that time?

LINNEY: Yes, I had a good agent at that time. But the issues I faced had nothing to do with having an agent or not. I was fortunate to have had some critically successful novels behind me. I was able to say, "Wait a minute." I'm sorry now, because it would have been a lot better if my first experience with a production and a director was a happy one. And then the bad experiences, which every writer and director have, would have been the exception rather than the rule. So anyway, it did work out fine. I kept writing plays and some novels and short stories. Two novels were just republished as well.

HYLTON: How did your television writing come about?

LINNEY: Well, my television writing career came about when my second daughter was born and I needed some money. I did some things for PBS and a thing about the history of Kansas for CBS. Once I got through my daughter's birth and paid the hospital bills and all that, I was gone. Because if you're going to do TV you have to hustle. You have to spend a great deal of your time doing that. And I didn't feel like spending my time hustling. I wanted to use my time to write my strange plays. I made one screenplay about a play of mine that was produced the most. It was called <u>Holy Ghost</u> and it was about Pentecostal snake handlers. It's been done as a play all over the country. It was sold as a screenplay that I wrote. They did not make it as a film at that point. About ten years later they called me back and said they wanted to renew the option on the screenplay and make a film, but I asked them to send me the script, whatever it was at that point. Because when the producer buys the script they then rewrite it. So they finally sent it to me and they changed everything around to exactly the way I did not want it. So I signed off and said, "No."

HYLTON: I was speaking with another writer recently about his work in film and television and he mentioned that the problem with film is that once you've written it and sold it, it is theirs.

LINNEY: Well, if you don't care about it that much it's fine. Take the money and forget it. But this particular play was done all over the country by many people. And many people love it. It's about Pentecostal snake handlers and it is not satirical. I have the greatest respect for these people. And, of course, the rewritten screenplay was turning the characters into morons. And that's not something that I wanted to be a part of.

HYLTON: Given your background with directors, how do you feel about the thought of the director as an editor?

LINNEY: Well, you have all kinds because there are all kinds of directors. I became a director because one of my plays was being done badly. It was a good play and so the producer and I sort of goaded the director into blowing his top. And so I directed myself, very simply. It was a very simple piece that he had made very complicated. And it was very successful. And it is one of my most successful one acts. Typically the plays that I direct, that I wrote, are my Appalachian plays. About a third of my plays are Appalachian plays. They have very simplified staging. I mean, I am not a person who wants to direct a complicated play like a Shakespearean play or a musical. I have no ambition to do that at all. But the Appalachian plays are best done very, very simply. Those I think I can handle. I do feel I work well with actors. I know how they think, having acted a bit myself. But that's the extent of my directing. [Recently there was] a play of mine in the Ensemble Studio Theater marathon. It [was] a one act. And the director there, a very fine young director named Carlos Ernesto [directed] the play. And he had some suggestions for me that were very good. And so I said, "Yes, fine." And so I incorporated some of his thoughts. Once the production was up and there were some things that were not right with the production, I said, "Hey Carlos…" and he said "Oh, ok." And so we collaborated very well. It was a fine collaboration.

You don't want complete creative control over your plays. What you want is approval of things. You don't want them to force choices on you that you will not like. But you certainly do want people to make suggestions to you. Curt Dempster and I have the greatest respect for one another. He for me as a writer and I for him as a producer and a director. So I have this lovely young director and I had some suggestions and Curt came and listened to me and we put them into effect. So, that's fine. What's not so fine, is it can be an absolutely irresistible impulse for some people. They have to rewrite the play that they are directing. It is up to the writer to decide if they want to let them do that. The playwright will have to decide at that point if they will accept the changes that the director wants to make or, in many cases, give up the production. And that is hard. It is especially difficult for a young playwright.

That's the difficulty right now. It's not that there are less opportunities for playwrights now. That's not the case. There are much, much more now. When I came to New York in 1958, there was Broadway and Off-Broadway was just beginning. There was some resident theater, but they were not doing new plays.

The secret to all of this is to write a good play. If you write a good play today, you can get it done somewhere. Either at a resident theater or Off-Off-Broadway or regionally. You can get it done. What is difficult to do is to write a good play today that is something that people would want to produce. I don't think that people would now want to produce my first play because historical dramas are totally out of fashion. But at the time they were not. It was a pretty good play and it was something that people were interested in at that time.

HYLTON: So studying the market becomes important if you're a young playwright writing to get produced.

LINNEY: Well, yes. It helps. But if you're going to write a good play it really has to come up out of your unconscious. It has to come up out of something that you really care deeply about. There's a lot of craft to it and to writing things in a way that is very different from writing a novel. But those things can be learned. What cannot be learned is recognizing what you really have to say. What is it that you really want to do. When you can put that together with what some theaters would want to produce then you are going to be o.k.

HYLTON: Let's say you have a new play. Would you first go to regional theater with it or aim for Off-Broadway?

LINNEY: It depends on the play. It depends on a lot of factors. I will let a play of mine be done almost anywhere, unless it's a brand new play. Then you want to be careful. They are all fine. It just depends on what it is and who is there. I had a great time at Ensemble Studio Theater and the Theater for the New City. And, of course, I was the first Playwright in Residence at the Signature Theater in New York. And that was absolutely wonderful. Some were Off-Broadway. Some were Off-Off-Broadway.

I don't think I'll ever be a Broadway playwright. I had one play done on Broadway and it did not work at all. It was The Love Suicide At Schofield Barracks. That was done in 1971 and it was done in regional theaters quite successfully and in the first season at the Signature Theater it was done quite well. The first Signature season was in 1991. I wrote the play for Herbert Berghof, who was very kind to me, called me up and said, "Come down and teach with me." So I did. While I was down there I got involved and wrote it. Herbert did a wonderful production of it at the small theater at H.B. Studios. In moving it to Broadway it just didn't work. Everybody meant well. Cheryl Crawford produced it. Everyone meant very well, but the play, as it was moved, did not come off. It's too bad we couldn't take the play from Hebert's production and move it to a small Off-Broadway Theater. It would have been fine [Off-Broadway].

HYLTON: How hard is it trying to sell something to Broadway these days?

LINNEY: Well, you don't even try.

HYLTON: So a play like John Patrick Shanley's, Doubt, is an anomaly?

LINNEY: That's correct. It was done Off-Broadway, much like Wit, and then got moved to Broadway. Proof, Wit, and Doubt were all wonderful plays that got moved. They combine everything that a playwright really cares about, with marketability. And it's taken John Patrick Shanley a long time. He's always had the energy and the confrontational stuff. But to get that together with the stuff that's so solid and far reaching as Doubt is, well, that's something else. But that all came from smaller theaters. The last new play that I can remember that anyone premiered on Broadway was M.Butterfly. People would flock to see that just for the subject matter. To do a play on Broadway and open it on Broadway, I don't know how. It's all musical comedies that are the attraction now. And the plays that are good either come from the resident theaters or from England.

HYLTON: I heard you quote Schweitzer once saying that "Inside every artist there is another artist looking to get out." You've acted in plays as well as written and directed theater. Do you feel that the other artist within you has gotten out or is there still something in there you want to explore?

LINNEY: That's always a mystery. But I think what Schweitzer said there is really true, that inside the artist there is another one. I have a very good friend who is a painter, Janet Fish. She is a very eminent American painter. When I first presented that idea to her, she nodded. And when you look to Bach you see you have the great composer, but there is also a painter in there. You can see his music. It is so clear. The views are there. The structure is so apparent. There is no other music that is as cogent and clear, as well as being religiously uplifting, and all of those magnificent things.

But there is also a painter or visual artist inside Bach. So that's kind of what I mean. And it's not something that you can pedantically explain, but most artists will sort of nod. Inside me as a writer there is an actor. That's what I was first and what I really do as a writer is throw myself into what I am doing. Vladimir Horowitz once said that when he played the piano he could think that he was inside the music looking out. You become a part of it. You don't worry about how to write once you become a part of it. You have to learn basic stuff, but you try to become a part of what it is you are trying to do. And the degree to which you become that thing that you are trying to be is what really counts.

HYLTON: When you teach playwrights what advice do you give them as you are about to send them into the world?

LINNEY: Each playwright is individual. And especially when you are working with a small group of playwrights, you get to know them all very well. There are some who there is nothing to be said about. You don't know what is going to happen to them. You can be wrong and they can be terrific down the line. You certainly can't predict. But the ones who you think that you can help, you try to maybe point out to them how they can help themselves. You can help a playwright, but it's no help to push them.

KENNETH LONERGAN

Kenneth Lonergan was born in the Bronx in 1962. He is the author of several screenplays including <u>Analyze This</u>, <u>Analyze That</u>, and <u>Margaret</u>. Ken was nominated for Academy Awards for Best Screenplay for <u>Gangs of New York</u> and <u>You Can Count on Me</u>. He won the Oscar for his screenplay for <u>Manchester By The Sea</u>, which he also directed. He also received the Sundance Grand Jury Prize for Drama for <u>You Can Count on Me</u>. Lonergan's plays have been produced on Broadway and internationally. His stag plays have been nominated for Drama Desk, Outer Circle, and Oliver Awards. His play <u>The Waverly Gallery</u> was nominated for the Pulitzer Prize.

Chapter Fourteen

Morning, New York City

HYLTON: Many young playwrights begin by sending out their plays as blind submissions to theaters. Could you tell me a bit about your early attempts to get your plays produced?

LONERGAN: I never had any luck sending anything out blind. I did it for a while but it was totally useless. Contests are a little bit better because they are looking for something they've never heard of before. But the odds are not so great. I was in the Young Playwrights Festival, which is a contest, in the first year they did the competition. And that was a good contest because it was a smaller field. You had to be between eight and eighteen to qualify. I was seventeen when I wrote the play and eighteen when the festival did the play. The play was called <u>Loraine's Children</u>. They published it in an anthology of their first year plays and it is pretty much out of print now. But I have it somewhere. It was ok. I didn't like the production very much, but the play was ok. It was done at Circle Repertory. The Young Playwrights Festival is still around but they work out of different theaters now. It's a really good group though.

I think it all boils down to knowing people. You make friends in the same business and then they do better than you. But now you know them and they can help you. So after the Young Playwrights festival I went to New York University. While at NYU, I got sent to London to be an intern at the Royal Court Theatre. And they commissioned a work from me. Nothing came of it, but I came back to the States and did a reading of the play. It wasn't produced, but the experience was great. I met a lot of people and, if I had wanted to continue the relationship, I could have maintained a relationship with a theater in London. It would have been a really good head start. I wouldn't have been a total outsider and I would have known lots of people. The basic principle at the theaters is, if you have a stack of scripts on your desk you're going to read the ones from someone you know, who you have to read, and you won't likely get to the ones of the people you don't know.

HYLTON: Can you tell me about your work at NYU?

LONERGAN: It was fine. I had some teachers who I liked and I met people I liked and it was great because that introduced me to Naked Angels [Theater Group]. And I don't know what kind of life I would have had without that group. Going into NYU I really didn't know anyone in the business. I had a few friends who were trying to be actors but that was it. I think it's very important to remember not to let your professional ambitions interfere with your artistic ambitions. Because I think it's bad for your writing, for the culture, and I don't think it's good to be writing plays that you think are going to go over well unless you are really smart about that. Most of the time that just leads to writing crappy plays and pandering. I always think it's important to keep those tracks separate.

Writing is nice to try and do for a living because you don't have to be hired to do it. You're not like an actor who can be paralyzed waiting for a role to be able to function. You can write all you want by yourself and have a parallel track where you're sending stuff out and networking and all of that stuff. And I was never really good at networking. But I learned to say "Hello" and be around and stay around and meet people who I wanted to help out and wanted to help me out as well.

HYLTON: How important was NYU for networking within the business?

LONERGAN: I made four friends at NYU, one of whom was really good at networking. Since I wasn't it was great because that person was able to help me along. And also I met friends who I worked with. But professionally it wasn't like I made all sorts of contacts. I just met a few friends who helped me out. But I wouldn't have met them if I had not gone to the school. I got to go to England [to the Royal Court] and had I been a person who was more likely to take advantage of those things at that time, I think that would have been a very good professional start for me. I met a lot of people at a real theater in London. I could have gone back and gotten something going in London but I just wanted to be here. And it never would have occurred to me to do that back then.

HYLTON: What was the experience like in London?

LONERGAN: It was a really good time. I was there for six months and I was exposed to this very different type of theater, which was this very political didactic theater that they think is so great. A lot of the plays were good and a lot of them were bad, but they were worthless in their minds if they were not about a public issue. I did not agree with that theory. But they feel that Americans are all obsessed with family drama, so I think the whole thing is not a real argument. I was just amazed that they'd do a play about lesbians on the island of Grenada and it would be dreadful, but because it was about lesbians on the island of Grenada when the United States was invading that would make the play. There could have been a better written, more interesting play that was not about a publicly charged topic and they would never look at it twice. I thought that was extremely stupid and I still do. But I also think that there wasn't anything wrong with trying to do plays on public issues if you want to do them. But they were really nice to me. I saw a lot of plays that I never forgot and it was a really great experience. That was back in 1985.

So after the Royal Court and NYU, I got involved, through my roommate, with the Naked Angels Theater Company. And that was the only place I was able to work for around eight years. And that was just a bunch of kids from NYU who all decided to form their own theater company. Which is a very good idea, in my opinion, but kind of hard to do. They had some people with big names who helped them get a certain profile for a while, but there were a lot of other young theater companies in town at the time. Still, I think that's a good way to do things. I don't think it's quite as effective to do things through showcases, just for professional reasons. I think you need to do plays for the sake of doing them well. If you [do that] and stick around it's not a very big community. Slowly you will edge in from the sort of really ratty out of the way theaters to the slightly better ones. And someone may be really good at raising money and may turn out to know someone who knows someone with the theater. It's all through personal connections as far as I can see. I think there are cases where people have dumb luck. I guess Julliard had a pretty good program because the classes graduate professionally and they know each other. And I believe Julliard has relationships with a variety of different theaters. But you have to get into the program.

If you succeed and get in, once you are in and you know each other you become a network of your own. As you start to grow it helps. I think it is possible to create your own network from scratch if you have people you want to work with. And in a way it's probably the better route, since you're really supposed to be figuring out what you want to do and not just trying to get hired. It's sort of a way to "make your own sauce," so to speak. And then people will go see plays because their friend is in a play or will go because their agent has to go. I know lots of people who are actors who got agents because they were in some teeny little show somewhere and some agent gave them a chance. And the truth of the matter is agents always need clients both for acting and writing.

There are always young agents who need new clients because the older agents have all of the clients at the agency. So I think it's very difficult especially if you make that first leap from outside of everything without having any "in" at all. But if you need to do it, you should rent a theater and put up a show.

Getting people there is difficult and that's a special skill that only a few people have, but you can start with smaller groups of people and eventually it does go somewhere. At least it has for a lot of people I know.

And it is easier for me to speak because I got very lucky after a long while and that's the way I came up. But there were other people who did exactly the same thing I did and did not end up in as nice a situation as I am in the moment. But I worked at it for almost ten years at Naked Angels. I couldn't get produced at any decent theater. And by that I mean any next step up theater like Playwrights Horizons or just name it. None of them would look at me. I was very fortunate to have Naked Angels for that ten year period to work on my material. There was sort of a feeling beyond the New York black box black tee shirt theater scene and I was very happy working there. And when I tried to get my work performed at other places it wasn't happening. So without Naked Angels I don't know what would have happened.

HYLTON: And Naked Angels was pretty new when you started working with them?

LONERGAN: I wasn't a founding member, but I came in the second year. I was one of the people who started the "Tuesdays at Nine" [reading series]. A bunch of us started it up and it's been a very successful program. They have to move [locations] all the time, because they don't have an actual home base. But I still go to that every once in a while. I find it very useful and it's a great place to meet people too. At first it was just us. We met and read little things to each other and actors read. There were always several outer circles of writers for Naked Angels who were not "worthy to be in the company, which was the ultimate honor." Those people provided most of the energy and did most of the work, despite having far lesser status. But there were always lots of people around. After a while people just started showing up. And all of these people who we never saw before started coming too. I didn't know where they came from, and I still don't. Now there's a website but it's gone on for so many years now. The quality of the work there is very variable. But there are some good things and you get some good writers and actors showing up from time to time. It's a really simple form and it's really helpful. It's all short so you don't have to listen to anyone for too long. You can be sure that it's going to be over in five to ten minutes.

HYLTON: What space were they using back then?

LONERGAN: Well, they had a home for a little while. Then they lost it. The home was a gift from the uncle of one of the members, which does not come along too frequently. They had a home for a while and then the lease ran out and they kicked us out. Unfortunately, soon after that time the company semi-dissolved. The focal point was gone and we'd been around for five to eight years and a lot of groups burn themselves out by that time. And Naked Angels partly burned itself out by that time, even though nobody really wanted to disband. But lots of people were in California and not around anymore. And we were renting spaces and that just took away the main focus of the group. Having a space is really important. But there are nice spaces to rent if you can get the money together. So they did full productions and readings and lots of one acts of my stuff.

HYLTON: How many plays do you think you'd done at that point?

LONERGAN: I'd done one full length production of a play and one workshop as well. I was involved in four or five "issues projects," which were four or five one acts all revolving around a certain theme. I was the co-writer on three big one evening only benefits. It was one thing we'd do back then to raise money. We'd have dozens of characters and five or six writers. Those were fun for us anyway. Then you know, there were lots of readings and workshops.

And then finally The New Group did, <u>This Is Our Youth</u>. And that play was a really good production. The New Group was really quite hot at the time. I was almost thirty and I had been trying to get plays produced for over ten years. I think I started trying when I was nineteen. And that was the only time when I sent a play in that the literary manager read it, had the artistic manager read it, they did a reading of it, and then they offered to do the play. I think that was the only time that ever happened. And it certainly was the only time that it ever happened with a group I wanted to work with. So that was ten years before that happened. Then I got really lucky because the play got a wonderful reception and suddenly I had a public profile, after ten years of having very little public profile.

The year after that pretty much any Off-Broadway theater I wanted would do a play by me. And I was the same person I was before that happened. The writing was the same, but that's how it worked. That was a little more unusual. My situation was a little more like what people fantasize about. But that one experience changed everything for me professionally.

HYLTON: How did you get the play read by the right people at the New Group?

LONERGAN: I knew an actress through Naked Angels who worked with them. And I don't think I would have been successful in getting the script to them had it not been for her. Getting a script to a literary manager is not the be all and end all anyway. It's usually the last stop. The literary manager reads it and if they're nice they call you up and give you some criticism, that you don't want, and that's how it happens. This artistic director (Scott Elliot) read it and liked it and that's how it got done. I had stopped sending in blind submissions years before because it never worked. And from that point on I felt pretty much like I could almost do whatever I wanted. And I guess The Waverly Gallery was done after that and that was done at The Promenade Theater. And after that Lobby Hero made it to Playwrights Horizons and then again at The John Houseman. And This Is Our Youth was done again a year later. And then, a few years later, both This Is Our Youth and Lobby Hero were done in London. That was great because now I have something of a career in London. But it's very odd. Work always does lead to work, sometimes.

In a way it's better if you just concentrate on doing what you are doing and hope that it leads to something. I had movie star friends. I did readings and showcases with them in the roles. It did nothing. Nobody ever came. I did a reading of this play that nobody ever really liked, except me. And I tried very hard to get it done for a couple of years. I couldn't get it anywhere. I had a hard time even getting Naked Angels to do it. And by the time they were ready to do it, I had lost interest in it because it had been so long since I had written the play. I would organize these readings and rehearse and only my friends would show up.

I had an agent in there somewhere and the agent didn't do me any good at all until I became successful on my own. And then they were right there, ready to help out. A playwright agent can't do that much. This may not be true of all of them. But in my experience my agent did nothing until I had gotten pretty far along myself. In my film work that is not true at all. In film I started out by getting an agent and the agent did shop the script around in ways that I couldn't have. But for plays it's not quite like that I think. Now I have two people, one for plays and another for film and they are different people from years ago. I shifted over the years. I think there's a small number of playwrights, a smaller number of theaters that take submissions at all, and the agents have relationships. For whatever reason I didn't get anything from the agent until I had made a name for myself.

Now, if I write a play I can be pretty confident that I can get it done. I won't get it done anywhere, but most anywhere that I want. I don't know for how long that will be true. But the agent isn't now so much for submitting the play, but more to give advice on producers to work with and just working on the details of the deal. It's not a question of submission anymore. This is especially true in New York. In regional cities I guess the agent does sort of shop your play around because you don't have time or know where to shop it. But that tends to be a play that was done in New York previously and is now moving on to another circuit. And you tend to not be as interested in that as you are in an initial New York production.

HYLTON: How much do you feel readings help you in your writing process?

LONERGAN: I used to do more readings in the past than I do lately. I always do one or two readings and it's usually better to do more than that. And sometimes you need to do a whole workshop of something. It's a little bit of a drag for me for some reason. I'm a little bit impatient now and I think it's good to do readings and workshops. At a certain point you just have to do a reading or you don't know anything. You learn so much more about what you're doing when you do a reading and you can hear it out loud. And once you've passed a certain point by yourself you just can't tell anything. Or at least I can't. So readings are just absolutely key. And I guess I always do a lot of rewriting. I don't like to do it but it just ends up happening. I try not to do too much once it's basically ok. But I tend to rewrite a lot.

HYLTON: I know that when This Is Our Youth was produced you had another director (Mark Brokaw) come in to direct the production. What's your feeling on directing your own plays?

LONERGAN: I didn't direct most of the stuff at Naked Angels on my own, although I did a lot of back seat driving. There is a very strong prejudice in theater against writers directing their own work. I think there's a prejudice because they think that writers are not very good directors, ignoring the fact that most directors are not very good directors. And I think it would have been nearly impossible for me to direct This Is Our Youth by myself, because of that conventional wisdom that writers should not direct their own work. And many of them shouldn't and most of them don't want to. But I had Mark Brokaw, who I work very well with, and he directed Lobby Hero. We worked together many times. So that worked out really well. Now if I wanted to direct a play I guess I could, but there still would be a little bit of a question about it I think. In the movie world, for no reason, either it seems cool and hip to have a first time director to write and direct his own stuff. It makes no sense.

It's possible that it's because a director in a movie can function only as a decision maker and everyone else will take care of everything else. He doesn't have to organize the schedule. He doesn't have to shoot the picture or edit the film. And that's somewhat true in theater but if there's a smaller group there's… Well, I don't know where the thought comes from, but with directing a movie it's a much bigger job than directing a play. I'm not sure it's a harder job, but it's definitely a much more daunting job in terms of what you have to do. I think theater direction is very elusive and you notice how elusive it is when playwrights try and direct their own work. If there's a director and a writer and someone doesn't like the show there's almost no way for someone to find out who did what.

Critics who have been reviewing plays for thirty years literally don't know the first thing about the components of a production. They don't know the first thing about what directors do and don't do and they almost always have it wrong whether it's a bad play and good director or a good play and a bad director. My parents are like, "What exactly do directors do?" And I said, "Well, it's really hard to answer." It's not like it's not a real job. It's extremely subtle and difficult. But it's a job you can do not one thing and if everybody else does their job you can end up looking great. You have to make some decisions. You have to cast this person and not that person and you have to not interfere if someone else is doing their job well. So you can't be a total non-participant, but you don't have to make a positive contribution if everyone else is doing their job.

HYLTON: Do you feel that it is helpful as a writer to direct what your write?

LONERGAN: I think it would have been helpful to direct because I ended up having to do it anyway, but I'd be there in the room with directors who I barely knew. I'd slowly realize that no director knew as much as I did about what I wanted with the play. None of them. Once in a while I'd meet someone good. And after a while I was like, "This is just stupid." In a way it's unfair too, because I clearly have more particular desires for the manifestation of this play. And it's unfair to do that and have someone else direct it and not call myself the director. Of course, Matt Brokaw was an exception and Matt Broderick directed some stuff of mine and he had a real contribution to make.

There are a couple of people who I really liked working with but, by and large, it just takes the gall to say you're a director, to become a director. You don't have to act or write. You just have to not be nervous telling people what to do and not to do. So you find yourself in these silly situations over and over again and realize that these people don't know anything. And you might as well do it yourself, since you're doing it all anyway. And they'll say, "Communicate to the actors through me." And you're like, "No, because you're not saying what I'm saying to them and they don't understand what you're saying and they understand what I'm saying." It depends. Many playwrights who I know who are very good writers just have no interest in directing at all. Still, it's not fair to be a very active backseat driver and have a director. If you're going to do it and get a director, you should let the director direct the play.

HYLTON: Do you have any other suggestions for young writers just starting out?

LONERGAN: I think playwrights should take acting classes so that they have some idea of what actors have to go through. And then I think all directors should have to take acting classes and take direction from directors. That should be mandatory and I think playwrights would be advised to do the same thing. You just learn so much about [the process]. Even if you do that you still don't actually get it, but you get a hint as to what an actor has to go through in order to perform a play. And I think that would be helpful to how you write and how you go about it all.

STEPHEN BELBER

Stephen Belber was born in Washington, DC in 1967. He graduated from the Julliard Playwriting Program and has written numerous plays which have been performed on Broadway, Off-Broadway, and regionally. He has received commissions from Manhattan Theater Club, Playwrights Horizons, and The Arena Stage. Stephen has written for televeision shows and several of his screenplays have been produced including Drifting Elegant, Tape, and Management, his directorial debut which premiered at the 2008 Toronto Film Festival. He Broadway produced play, Match, was made into a film in 2014.

Chapter Fifteen

Afternoon, New York City

BELBER: I did a lot of acting in high school. In college I was trying to be a novelist and doing a lot of prose writing. I wrote a novel when I got out of school and went to work and, somewhere along the line, I realized I missed acting. At which point I started writing one-person shows that I would perform. It was a way to combine the two. I was living in Washington, DC and working at the Hard Rock Café. I was living, working, and doing these shows at night. Eventually, when I was twenty-five, I decided that if I wanted to take this seriously I had to move up to New York. Once there I started taking night classes in playwriting at Playwrights Horizons Theater School. It wasn't particularly hard to get into, but it was a great program with great teachers.

Eventually I wrote and started doing a one-man show downtown in New York. The first one I did, when I moved to New York, was at CBGB's at CB's Gallery. I performed it on Monday nights and split the door [with the Club]. I would just invite my friends, which was sort of pathetic, but you have to start somewhere.

Somewhere along the line I became aware that Julliard had started [the Playwrights] program. I applied to, what I believe was, the second year of the program and I was accepted. I had already applied once. [Julliard] tries to take the playwrights soon after college. So I was in my mid-to-late twenties, I guess. It's not a masters degree. You don't pay. You have these weekly seminars with [Marsha Norman and Christopher Durang]. And you have access to the Julliard actors, the Julliard library, the cafeteria, and you eventually, if you are lucky, get a full production and lots of little productions. So there's no obligatory reading, no syllabus, and no compelled work as you would have with a masters at Columbia or such.

But it was probably the first time that I started really getting into reading a lot of plays. They had a great library and I basically learned to take myself seriously as a writer. Julliard gives you access to a real venue and actors who are extremely talented. And you can read your work the day after you write it if you want. Every Saturday you have the actors at your disposal and you get criticism once a week and you can sit in on various classes. I think Michael Kahn started that whole playwriting arm to create a web of relationships between actors, directors, and writers who could then go out in the world together. And it has completely worked in my eyes.

HYLTON: What would you say is the biggest benefit of this type of program?

BELBER: I would say for me it was really just having tremendous actors at my disposal. Rather than having to call up people and beg them to come over to my living room, Julliard provided casting help with anything I wrote and would then invite a pretty distinguished crowd to see the readings.

HYLTON: And from a contact/career standpoint...

BELBER: Contact wise it was great. There are a lot of actors I still work with and I can call them up now and say, "Will you do my reading?" or "Would you come over and read this for me?" I think the three other writers in the program with me at Julliard came out with an agent afterwards.   I didn't at first, which was quite distressing. They give you a showcase at the end of each year to invite industry people and you definitely feel the pressure. When I got out of the program I was highly aware of what was going on in the professional world in a way that it's very easy to become jealous because suddenly you're aware of who has an agent and all of that. But you get over it because that's the way the game works.

HYLTON: So before getting an agent how did you get your work seen by theaters?

BELBER: I was basically pounding major pavement. I bought The Dramatists' Sourcebook. The SoHo Rep [production] came about because I was trying to coproduce a lot of stuff, which really meant hustling around town to get people to let me use their space. My wife was directing a lot of my work. We would do something and then someone from SoHo rep would come and say, "Hey, do you want to do that in a late night slot?" So I was applying like hell to all of these programs around the country and sending scripts to places Off-Broadway like Manhattan Theater Club and Second Stage on my own. It was brutal.

If I could get reimbursed for some of that stuff, for my ten years of sending out those scripts, I'd be a millionaire. It was kinda dumb. But, I literally sent scripts everywhere. I tried to send one or two a week and follow up with calls.

And the theaters just get annoyed. Because I know my writing wasn't up to par at that point and I'm sure I bugged these people. I see them around town now and they walk the other direction. They think I'm going to give them a script out of my pocket. And the agents are so harsh. I spent a really long time trying to get an agent and I'm sure that without Julliard, I still wouldn't have one.

HYLTON: Did you send out full scripts or samples to theaters?

BELBER: Depends on what [the theaters] were willing to read, and what their rules were for submissions. But mostly I wouldn't hear back. And even when I had an intro from a friend of a friend, it didn't work. I tried to get friends' agents to read my stuff for a few years and I think it worked once. It's tricky.

HYLTON: So if you had a suggestion to make to young writers aspiring to get produced right now what would it be?

BELBER: I would think that if you can get your work into little theaters, even if not a lot of people see it, it's worthwhile because it does create a foundation of relationships that are fun and useful. Even if it's like the guy who was running your lights one night ends up being a hot agent at CAA. I also think it's the best way to make your work better. I know that the eight or nine years of pounding the pavement and doing shows and doing readings made me not only better but also able to sculpt my work, write on the run, and understand how to say what I wanted to say. Basically it compelled me to hone my craft.

HYLTON: What about self-marketing?

BELBER: I'm always so afraid of being obnoxious, so there were times I simply wouldn't follow up for fear of offending. But that's just a judgment call based on your personality. What's important is that the work is the priority. That is easy to forget sometimes. You have to send out a really good piece, because that will do the talking for you. So I guess, my overall suggestion would be to make sure that your craft is the priority and the submissions are secondary.

HYLTON: Did any of your productions come from blind submissions?

BELBER: Not really blind submissions. The only one that worked was this one cutting edge theater that I found through The Dramatists' Sourcebook. I won the second prize in their competition. And that was the one thing that I can point to that paid off from the blind submission process. And I have an ongoing relationship with the theater now, which is nice.

HYLTON: What can you tell me about your experience with The Death of Frank at the Fringe Festival in New York?

BELBER: It's a great [Festival]. It's a lot of work and it's not always incredibly well organized, but for what they are doing it's amazing. The experience with The Death of Frank at the Fringe taught me a ton about how that play worked. And it's the one play of mine that a lot of the downtown publications, like Time Out and The Village Voice, liked, because it was a dark piece that no one was going to do uptown. People still refer to that play in their reviews. In fact, I think when Time Out came to review Match they were like, "Too bad he couldn't do what he did in 1999." So, they like dark. But the Fringe is incredibly helpful. It costs what, three hundred bucks and you have to pay for the lighting person--- but in the end it's more than worth it.

HYLTON: How does having an agent change your submission process at this point?

BELBER: I can't tell. It's obviously great to have that on your side. I always delude myself into thinking, "Oh, I've met a producer. They'll check out my work." But I think it's still better coming from an agent. Like these guys who did Match. I knew them, we're good friends, actually, but they sort of blew me off for a couple of years until I submitted through an agent, with Frank Langella attached. And the agent can also get actors attached. So agents do help, although now I feel I have developed more relationships. I feel I can call people and say "Will you read my script?" But the agent knows more people than I know. He spends his day building those relationships.

HYLTON: I know you have stuff coming up in Hartford and Huntington. Are you still applying for those kinds of things on your own?

BELBER: Those two no. Those were requests, which was nice. The O'Neill I still apply to and occasionally New York Stage and Film at Vassar and the Sundance Theater Lab. I applied for eight years to the O'Neill and finally got in last year. I went and Lee Blessing, who it seems has an open invitation to the place, came up to me and was like "Hey man, you should come up more often." And I was like, "I've fuckin' been trying." He's an excellent guy. My wife is directing a world premiere of his this summer in West Virginia.

HYLTON: What has been your experience with Naked Angels?

BELBER: I didn't have any real relationship with them in the past. I knew someone who was a founder and that's how Tape came about. She said, "This would be great for our company" and she attached Geoffory Nauffts, who was also a founding member and ended up directing it. A long time ago I had gone to the "Tuesdays at 9" readings that they do and I remember being highly intimidated by it. I submitted for the readings and never got picked. It's a great organization. I saw Kenny Lonnergan reading the first act of This Is Our Youth, when it was a ten-minute play. It was cool.

HYLTON: What was your experience with the Humana Festival?

BELBER: Tape went out there, after the downtown production of it with my buddies. That was great because, more than anything I had done to that point, it made me semi-legitimate as a writer. It is just a great festival. And I think you can still submit blindly to Humana. I had almost gotten in, with a play, a couple of years before that. And I remember thinking "If I get into this, I've got it made." And it's true, you get tons of productions, get published, and people around the world read the play and decide that they may want to do it. So it really is a good festival.

HYLTON: Can you tell me a little bit about the difference of being on Broadway (as with <u>Match</u>) versus being in smaller venues? I ask this because your plays seem frequently to have a smaller cast and make use of a small space.

BELBER: I don't think <u>Tape</u> would ever have worked on Broadway. But although <u>Match</u> has only three characters, it feels bigger because the topic is bigger. <u>Tape</u> was about ambiguity and minutia whereas <u>Match</u> just feels like a bigger play and thus inhabits the larger space better. I've been accused of <u>Match</u> being a sentimental play. Which is true. I'm a sentimental guy. And maybe Off-Broadway is a better space for more subtle material. If <u>Tape</u> is characterized as anything, it has to do with the human inability to perfectly put your finger on something. And in <u>Match</u> you can definitely put your finger on something, very precisely, but it doesn't necessarily get you where you want to go. It's less obscure, but maybe a little more accessible. <u>Match</u> is about larger forces and has bigger themes in terms of family and art and the loneliness that can creep in as life gets longer.

HYLTON: Did you write <u>Match</u> knowing that it was going to a large venue?

BELBER: Yeah, as soon as I knew that I was writing about this particular character, the one played by Frank

Langella who was inspired by someone in my life, I realized I was heading toward more commercially viable territory. And my normal instinct was to run away from that. But this time I decided, "Ok, this could be fun, let's see where it goes."

I had a friend who had just acted with Richard Chamberlin in The Sound of Music, on Broadway. And she was like, "Richard Chamberlin is looking to do a play. You should write something for him. It'll take you two weeks." And so I had that in my mind for a while. Then I met this guy in real life, who was such a big, beautiful, complex character and I thought "Ahh, I could get Richard Chamberlin to play that." So I came up with a story around him. And my friend actually gave it to Richard Chamberlin and he passed on [the script] saying it was too many lines.

But the husband of the woman who was in The Sound of Music, a great actor named Rob Lunney knew Frank Langella vaguely and he got him a script through Austin Pendelton. And Frank Langella called me up and said, "You wrote this part for me but you didn't even realize it." And he started helping me get producers attached basically.

HYLTON: So, you were involved very early on.

BELBER: Yeah, it was nice because we went to one producer but it didn't work out. And then the Araca Group picked it up. The guys in the group are my age and six or seven years earlier we had all done a show together off, Off-Broadway. So it was nice to get the script to them.

Ray Liotta was a thing where a lot of names were being thrown about. And people were saying, "We need a star, we need a star." I came up with his name because he had that type of star quality I thought they were looking for, but also because he was perfect for the part. And so many times when you're looking for star quality you sacrifice that. My Dad had some movie index guide and I looked under all people in that age. I went through it page by page until, "Oh fucking Ray Liotta." And luckily we got him, despite it not being as big a part as Frank's, although it is just as vital. I think [Ray] had a personal connection to it and he was the first person we went to.

HYLTON: Were you involved in the production after it got to the director?

BELBER: Yeah, I was, since it had never been done before. There was a lot of rewriting. In fact, Ray Liotta had some very strong opinions that were really helpful. He gave me ideas that I hadn't thought of that were really fresh. Frank had been involved and we had actually done a three-day workshop a year [before]. So we were all sort of blind to something and Ray came in and helped us figure it out in a very astute way. So there was a lot of rewriting in rehearsal and during the three weeks of previews we did a lot. It was pretty hardcore.

HYLTON: Have you involved the actors in the rewriting process of other plays you have written?

BELBER: We workshopped Tape Off-Broadway and did a production of it. And I would get together with all three actors (Dominc Fumusa, Josh Stamberg, and Phoebe Jonas) because I was particularly close with them. We changed the script constantly. It was so early and we really had no idea at times what the play had to say. So fine-tuning was a fun part of that. That's one skill I have sort of developed a little bit. I go slower now, listen to the actors, make adjustments on the script, and go with the flow a little more.

HYLTON: What do you like in terms of a relationship between yourself and a director?

BELBER: I like a director who pushes me hard and tells me to articulate and understand why I've written certain things. Because I think I write out of instinct a lot. I know if something feels good or sounds nice, but sometimes I have to make sure I can back it up with a reason. And Nicky Martin is a good example of someone who forces me to explain what I really want to say.

HYLTON: You mentioned that your friend said it would only take you a couple of weeks to write Match. How long does it take you to write your plays? I ask because I heard that by 1998 you had twenty plays produced in New York, with six produced in 1998 alone.

BELBER: Well, I don't know about that, but yes, that was a particularly good year. I'm sure it's a flaw because none of them are particularly historically important documents. I envy these guys who write one every three years and it's a masterpiece. So I do worry about that. But that being said I do like to sit and crank it out - at least the first draft. And as I said, I like to write on instinct, which means that sometimes I write twenty pieces and am lucky if one of them happens to hit a chord with people. So I am trying to learn how to take my time a little bit. But Match was quick. I went out to dinner with this man, who inspired the role, and he made such a profound impression on me that I immediately came home and scribbled down the anecdotes he'd just told me, many of which are in the play. So, once I had that, and once I'd figured out the plot framing, I literally wrote it in less than a week.

HYLTON: Do you know what's going to happen at the end of the play when you start writing?

BELBER: Often not. In <u>Match</u> I had a story and knew essentially where I wanted to go with it. <u>Tape</u>, yes, but some of the stuff in it was much more organic. But please know that I hate to use that word. In <u>Match</u> some of the smaller details I found along the way. But I hit upon that story fairly early and even though I thought I knew it was a simple story, I felt it deeply. It hit a chord with me and I was emotionally attached to it and had good luck with it.

HYLTON: Which writers inspire you?

BELBER: Albee is a big influence. He goes darker than I go in <u>Match</u>, but his writing is a huge influence in general. In terms of <u>Match</u>, I purposely let myself go into a classic, conventional sort of, almost parloresque type of drama to see what I could do with that. I'm sure the ones that don't get produced are trying to be more like Tom Stoppard. Sam Shepard was a huge influence, Caryill Churchill, Arthur Miller, Peter Barnes, Thornton Wilder, Eric Bogosian, and Stephen Adley Guirgis. All these folks have profoundly shaped my work.

HYLTON: Congratulations on <u>Management</u>, your film writing/directing debut. What can you tell me about the film?

BELBER: Management is a film I'm extremely proud of on many levels. It may not be for everyone, but it is entirely part of my self-proclaimed mission to bring well-rounded, oddly true and theatrically grounded characters to the screen. Management began as a one-act play, and thus, like Tape, Drifting Elegant, The Laramie Project and, hopefully soon, McReele and Match, it went through a genesis from stage to film that felt organic and strong, becoming better and learning more what it and its characters wanted to say along the way. It has, without a doubt, made me want to direct more movies, for it is an incredibly exciting and hugely satisfying way to chase the fulfillment of one's vision from A to Z.

NILO CRUZ

Nilo Cruz was born in 1960 in Mantanzas, Cuba. He graduated from Miami-Dade Community College where he studied theater. Nilo studied under playwright, Maria Irene Fornes in New York City prior to earning a degree in playwriting at Brown University. In 2003 Nilo won the Pulitzer Prize for his play, <u>Anna In The Tropics</u> which was moved to Broadway after its initial run at The New Theatre in Coral Gables, Florida. Nilo is a member of the New Dramatists and has had many plays produced regionally and Off-Broadway.

Chapter Sixteen

Afternoon, New York City

CRUZ: I moved to New York in 1988 to study with Maria Irene Fornes. I met Irene in Miami when I was directing a play of hers called Mud, and she was invited by a professor of mine to conduct a playwriting workshop at a local college where I was a student. Based on the work I did in her workshop, she invited me to be a part of the writing lab she used to head at INTAR Theater in NY. So basically I studied with her for three years.

HYLTON: What was it like studying with Irene?

CRUZ: Irene is very much into the process of visualization for playwrights. She doesn't want you to be judging the writing while it's being created. She's interested in expanding your mind, the world of the imagination, and entering that place and getting in touch with the subconscious. That's very much her approach. At INTAR we would read our plays aloud and she'd give us feedback based on the work. She's an excellent mentor who really concentrates on the creative process. She's a facilitator who helps writers get in touch with their unique and individual voice. Then, much later, I also had the good fortune of studying with Paula Vogel and Aisha Rahman at Brown University.

At Brown we read and discussed a lot of plays and our own work as playwrights. The main class, the workshop class, was geared towards the work of the individual writer. For me Brown was like a laboratory where you could write and come up with your own material and get excellent feedback from the other graduate students and professors. My experience there allowed me to take two years and come up with a body of work and be in an environment that nurtured the plays.

A playwright needs to get to know his craft, and the only way to develop your voice as a writer is through the work. When I was at INTAR, every day we met from nine to twelve and we wrote scenes or monologues. It was like a job and we got paid for it. This is how I got to know my craft as a playwright, by sitting down everyday and doing the work, by disciplining myself, and not just waiting for the muse to appear.

Once you have found your voice as a playwright, and you feel confident about your work, you start sending your plays out into the world. When I was at Brown, I submitted my work to a lot of festivals including the Bay Area Festival in San Francisco. One of my plays was read at the festival and was later chosen by the Magic Theater as part of their next season. My first play on a professional stage was at the Magic Theater.

HYLTON: How did that opportunity happen?

CRUZ: It was through Paula Vogel. She suggested that I apply to the Bay Area Festival. It is very competitive, so I was very lucky to get in. I actually was very fortunate, since I participated in that festival three years in a row... talk about luck. After I finished Brown I kept writing plays. I was not interested in using my degree to get a teaching position or a corporate job. I just wanted to be a writer, even if it meant being poor and having to struggle in the material world. But somehow there was divine intervention. I was blessed when I was accepted into New Dramatists in New York. I had just graduated and I got in. New Dramatists is one of the few institutions in this country devoted to playwrights. It is like a studio or a sort of atelier for the work we do as writers. They offer playwrights residence for seven years, and that means having a place to do stage readings, which are essential for our process. You have access to professional actors and directors, and much more.

HYLTON: And connections no doubt?

CRUZ: Oh yes. Absolutely.

HYLTON: Did most of the people in the program with you have MFAs?

CRUZ: No, it was a mix. The members were a combination of writers who had been writing for a long time and then some less experienced writers...

HYLTON: What was the impact of New Dramatists on your work?

CRUZ: It was wonderful to be around other playwrights and to attend the readings. I got to meet many writers, not only local authors, but playwrights from England, Australia, Israel, and Canada. The exposure to all these different voices was quite fascinating. I basically lived at

214

New Dramatists. I didn't have much money when I moved New York. I was working at a bookstore and with the amount of money I made it was impossible to live in this city. So New Dramatists had a space upstairs that they were not using. It was a sound booth. Very little. So I asked them, "Do you mind if I use this space? I'll fix it up." I lived there for two years... basically three. I wanted to be a playwright and this allowed me to do my work and not worry about financial pressures. It was uncomfortable at times. Basically, I had to climb a little ladder to get to my room. It was hard to concentrate at times, especially when actors were rehearsing for a reading of a play or a musical. But I adjusted to the environment and the life of the place. I couldn't ask for more. I was extremely grateful to New Dramastists.

There were days I would go out and read or work elsewhere and come back at night, and maybe tried to do more writing when it was quiet. Then there were days that I had the whole place to myself. It was wonderful to feel the energy of the building because there's something sacred about this place, since it used to be a church. I think of it as a sort of temple for playwrights. Yes, I can't deny the Catholic influence in me. I was extremely happy there. Actually, as child I always wanted to live in a church. This doesn't mean that I wanted to be a priest. No thank you. But there's a part of me that's attracted to a sacrosanct atmosphere.

HYLTON: I think your story gives a real reality check for young writers about the industry and the ongoing challenges one may face despite being professionally produced.

CRUZ: Yes, it's a choice we make as playwrights and there's a price to pay. But I'm not one to complain. I'm like a horse with blinders. I just look straight ahead. I'm interested in the work, the process, and my hope is that the plays will eventually be produced. I count my blessings. Inspiration is a blessing, the fact that we can dream up characters and create a whole world different than our own. All in all, I've been lucky. By the time I was out of graduate school Paula Vogel was kind enough to help me find an agent. So when I graduated I had representation and that's very helpful.

HYLTON: So you didn't have to go through the mass mailing stage that many young playwrights experience?

CRUZ: I did, in graduate school and somewhat when I was at New Dramatists.

HYLTON: When you were in graduate school and were sending things out how did you decide where you would send your material?

CRUZ: I used the Dramatists' Sourcebook and Paula guided me too. She was excellent at giving us advice. She is a working playwright and that's the benefit of studying with a working playwright. They have experience with theaters. They have connections. It was the same with Irene Fornes.

HYLTON: At what point in the development of a play do you do readings or send out your material?

CRUZ: I think it's important that the play has some sort of completion. I usually send it out after the third of fourth draft. It's not good to send a play out too early in its development. You don't want it to end in the pile of incomplete plays.

HYLTON: Do you tend to rely on readings or smaller productions to assess the state of your writing?

CRUZ: Readings are important because they give you a sense of where you are in the process, and what you need to do in order to take the play to the next level. It's also good to read the script in front of an audience and see how well the play is operating, feel the vibe in the room. But readings and workshops can only do so much for a play. We have to remember that we are not just telling a story through words but also through a set, lights, and a group of actors and a director. A production would be better, of course, because that's when you get to see all of the elements come together.

HYLTON: It's interesting to hear you say that because in the interviews I've read with you and after seeing and reading Anna In The Tropics, I think one of the comments about your work is that it is so lyrical and that it can very nicely exist, and perhaps thrives, on the page as much as it does on the stage. It is poetry.

CRUZ: I believe my play was chosen for the Pulitzer based on the way it was written on the page without being seen in New York.

HYLTON: Which is amazing.

CRUZ: But it is also the way that it should be done. A director can enhance a play through a production.

HYLTON: So the play may be weak and yet it wins based on the director and actors?

CRUZ: Yes. We have to remember that the theater is an interpretive art form and plays can be interpreted in many different ways.

HYLTON: Once you've started writing a piece do you go directly to readings with it or not?

CRUZ: Yes, because to me language for the stage is rhythmic and I want to see how the language is operating and what story I am telling. And again, theater is interpretive and it comes to life in a third dimension.

HYLTON: I know you say that music is instrumental to your work. Do you listen to something in particular when you write?

CRUZ: I listen to all kinds of music. I pay attention to the structure of music, because I feel a theater piece must have the same kind of movements and variety of rhythm that music offers. I don't make a habit of listening to music when I write, because I respond to music in an emotional way, and there has to be a balance between logic and emotion when you are writing. Besides, English is my second language and I feel I need to make sure that what I write makes sense in the English language. Most of my characters are Latinos and I'm interested in capturing their sensibility, and the way they express themselves. This doesn't mean I'm translating. No, not at all! What I'm trying to do is to illustrate the essence of my characters, the inflections, and the musicality of their emotional life through words.

Sometimes I have to restructure certain lines, because I catch myself writing things that perhaps don't make any sense in the English language. And that's because most of my characters think in Spanish, but through the writing they express themselves in the English language. Sounds bizarre, doesn't it? But again, I don't believe I am translating. I am trying to arrest a certain kind of sensibility that defines a particular ethnic group of people. For instance, when I am reading a book in the English language I am not translating each word from English to Spanish. On the contrary, I have an understanding of the language, because I studied it.

HYLTON: Have you written any plays in Spanish? And would you do that?

CRUZ: No. I've always been interested in American theater and if I limited myself to Spanish theaters I would be very limited in my potential venues, at least in this country. I could take my plays to Latin America, but in Latin America playwrights are secondary and it is a director's world. In the United States and in England the voice of the playwright still has some validity and resonance. More than anything I educated myself in this country.

HYLTON: There was a lot of buzz about you when you won the Pulitzer since your work was first performed outside of New York.

CRUZ: There are great theaters outside of New York that do wonderful work, and it's a shame that they don't get the recognition they deserve. Doing a play on Broadway is not necessarily about having a good script. It's about so many other things. It's about getting a group of famous actors, perhaps celebrities…. It's a very commercial industry.

HYLTON: When you were down in Florida I understand you directed plays. How was it that you got into directing?

CRUZ: I had a professor who guided me in that direction. I believe a playwright needs to have an understanding of directing and the collaborative process that is involved in dialoguing with actors and designers, the overall complexity that is involved in staging a production. It can only help you to be a better playwright.

HYLTON: Do you feel as though your submission process has changed now that you have an agent and success on Broadway?

CRUZ: I still get rejection letters. But I don't believe that has anything to do with my work. Sometimes theaters are looking for specific things for their seasons. They might want to balance the work that they are presenting and my script isn't appropriate for that season or for their theater. There are many playwrights out there and theaters can only produce so many plays, so I don't let these rejection letters discourage me.

I encourage young playwrights to send their work to theater festivals. It's a good way of getting exposure. Festivals like the Bay Area in San Francisco, the Public Theater Festival, and the Pacific Playwrights Festival at South Coast Repertory are all fantastic. I remember being at the Bay Area Festival and a play of mine, <u>Dancing On Her Knees</u>, was being read there. And Morgan Jenness from the Public Theater was at that festival. She came back to New York and told George Wolfe about me, and that's how I was able to get my first production in New

York. A year later I became a writer in residence at the Public.

It's a blessing when you have the support of a theater like the Public or a place like New Dramatists, where you can do your work and develop your craft. As I said before, writing is about developing your voice. Playwriting is about rewriting and rewriting a script until you have captured a handful of life on the page. I didn't know how to do rewrites until I wrote my fourth play. It takes a long time to learn the art of rewriting. For some reason we hold on to certain details, the same way we hold on to life. Maybe it is because there is violence and destruction in the rewriting process. You have to shift things around, or you have to remove certain details and replace them with new life. The truth is you have to be ruthless and perform what I call surgery.

HYLTON: How did you learn to perform surgery?

CRUZ: It's a difficult task. It can be quite messy. With every script it's different. The most obvious reason is when a play still feels like an idea that hasn't been fully fleshed out. But you have to be aware of the musicality of the script and that you don't lose the syncopation of the rhythms.

HYLTON: It seems very hard to know as a writer when to change things. I think Romulous Linney said something like "There are three things innate in everyone. They want food, they want sex, and they want to rewrite someone else's play."

CRUZ: That's true most people want to rewrite our plays. But I believe writers are listeners, and we have to learn what to listen for when others offer their criticism.

More than anything, we have to listen to the specific voice of the play we are trying to write.

HYLTON: It seems clear that you benefited on multiple levels from your work at Brown and from your relationship with Paula Vogel. I wonder what you think the value of the pedigree is to the student?

CRUZ: Studying for the arts should never be about the pedigree of a program or the prominence of a university. It should be about the craft and nothing else. You can actually study on your own and not be part of an institution. Writing for the theater is about observing life and tapping into the subconscious, into the essence of dreams and distilling human behavior into needs and actions.

NEIL LaBUTE

Neil LaBute was born in Michigan in 1963. He received his B.A. from Brigham Young University. Neil studied in graduate theater programs at the University of Kanas and New York University. LaBute has enjoyed numerous Off-Broadway and regional productions of his plays. He has also become famous for his film productions, which began with his Sundance Award winning film, <u>In the Company of Men</u> (1997). He won the Cannes Film Golden Palm Award in 2000 for his direction of the film, <u>Nurse Betty</u>. Since then Neil has had many plays and screenplays produced and remains dedicated to working on the stage. His play <u>Reasons To Be Pretty</u> was produced on Broadway in 2009 and was nominated for the Tony Award for Best Play.

Chapter Seventeen

Morning, Los Angeles

LABUTE: For me there was no great push towards the theater. There was no one influential person. There was no being taken to the theater all the time and it being part of my life as a kid. I saw pretty standard school plays. With my brother being older, I would occasionally go to the odd play with him at his college. I'd also go to the local community theater. There was, however, some connection with what I did see that made sense to me. I had some reaction to the live performance and I said to myself, "I like what's happening there." In junior high there was probably a drama class that I took as well. I don't think we even did productions in junior high, there was just a single performance course. But in high school it started happening to me. It always comes down to a good instructor. I had a great instructor in my junior and senior years. His name was Terry Parker and he was doing interesting shows. He just had a way of whipping the whole department into shape. He got us into statewide competitions and things that were interesting. I didn't grow up in an area where I was privy to great material. I couldn't run down to the Spokane Public Library and find all the new plays. So there was a point where I started writing my own stuff. I would write a monologue and then I'd try to slip it past him. I'd put some name on it and see if I could sneak it by as the work of some author from New York. And usually I did. I then wrote a scene for some people in a competition and that carried me over to college.

Brigham Young was almost a mirror of how I grew up. They weren't that interested in new material. They sent [students] back to the classics. But in college [I got involved with the] American College Theater Festival (ACTF), and, I have to say, my whole career is built on the ACTF. You had to get permission from any living authors to do their work and you had to bring the letters with you [when you would put on another playwright's play]. But if it was something you wrote you could bring it right with you. So it was no hassle [to do your own work]. And this was before email and all of that. So it was a pain in the ass to send a letter off. So I was the go-to guy who could write quick, funny, interesting scenes. In college I was writing a lot of short sketches and comedy stuff. My ideal at that time was to get onto Saturday Night Live, so I spent a lot of time doing that and other theater work. Every so often in a theater I'd do a collection of sketches and make a show out of it.

So when I first graduated I came to New York with a bunch of sketches and thought, "How am I gonna get onto Saturday Night Live? It's impossible to even get in the door." Somebody I knew, with whom I went to Brigham Young, worked for an art dealer, and this art dealer had this amazing Rolodex filled with big names. Lorne Michaels was one of the names in that Rolodex. So I was like, "Dude, give me that number." One Sunday, I built up my courage and called [Lorne] at home. Unbelievably, he answered the phone, and I was like, "Look, I know this is weird, but this is what you have to do sometimes. I know I'd be great for your show and it's impossible to get to you so I figured I'd just try you at home. And you may not like it but you gotta give me marks for trying. Would you just take a look at my material?" And he basically said, "Don't call me at home. Get an agent or whatever, but don't call me at home." And I ran into him years later and he actually heard about it and it made him laugh. And he was like, "Of course I remember."

Anyway, I'd moved to New York post undergrad and I was bumming around thinking I was going to do some plays and just get something going. Then a friend of mind decided to go to graduate school and I thought to myself, "You know, I should have a terminal degree," just in case this doesn't happen I should at least be able to teach it and keep my hands in it that way. I like teaching. So, I went to Kansas to get a masters and spent a couple of years there. They had a good library and I got into British Theater. I would check out like twenty books at a time, and I'd just read and read everything I could. I'd do plays all over campus. There was an explosion of theater there. I met really good actors. That's where I met Paul Rudd. Still, even after I graduated from there I was thinking I had to get a PhD.

So around 1990 I went to Chicago for a little while. I started to taste the theater scene there, which has always been good, and I figured I would send out a couple of PhD applications. I got into NYU's program and figured, "I better take this. This will be good." And it was good and bad but it was in New York, so I was around a lot of theater. I had really good teachers. You got to meet really good people, no matter what the department politics turned out to be.

HYLTON: Did you get production opportunities through NYU's program?

LABUTE: Yes, but again it was pretty much my own muscle. If I couldn't get one production at a place I wanted, then I'd go out and rent a space and do one myself. I wasn't big on being told "No." I'd move on and make it happen on my own. I thought that I would get a lot of contacts out of NYU, but what I found was it was a very insular program. Writers stayed with the writers and directors stayed with directors, and all of the filmmakers wanted to do everything on their own films. So I wasn't writing films for anyone. That was a bit of a let down. But I did meet writers who I've remained in contact with and teachers who are now friends. I've also gone back and taught there. Because of the nature of the place, it felt very competitive so I think I wrote with a type of speed and excitement because of the nature of that atmosphere. That was a very good for me. I got my first agent out of it and I got a reading at the SOHO Rep.

There was a period where one of my teachers got hired on a short lived Fox Television Show, and all of these interesting actors were on the show, like Oliver Platt, Stanley Tucci, and Mandy Patinkin. It was a New York-based comedy set in this apartment building called Urban Anxiety. I was hired as a student to come write for them because this teacher liked what she saw in my work. I was actually writing for them while I was in school and I was able to join the Writer's Guild. So from that perspective, lots of good things happened [while at NYU].

I think you make your own destiny in many ways. The fact that I go off and do theater as often as I do drives my agents nuts. They're like, "Holy crap. Don't you know what's important in life." And I say, "Actually, yeah, I do." To me, it's hugely important to return to the theater on a regular basis.

The last semester I was at NYU I did an exchange program to The Royal Court in London. I was in the literary department just reading plays and I got to shadow people within the Royal Court. It was a very interesting time.

I used to look at The Dramatists Sourcebook and I would do cold submissions to festivals all over the country. I received tons of letters saying "No thank you." I also did a cold submission to Sundance Playwrights Lab and I got in. That sealed the deal on going back to Brigham Young for the PhD. Good things came from that festival. They have a set cast of actors they bring up and cast in your show, so you can work on it and read it in the beginning and it culminates in another reading at the end. But [Sundance] didn't push [your play] towards product. We were the audience for everyone else's plays. It was more, "How can we make this better?" Stacy Edwards was in my play there. She ended up in my film [In The Company Of Men] when I decided to make the movie, five years later. Each moment at Sundance has led to something else equally wonderful.

I actually wrote a screenplay of my film for someone else, which they decided not to do. And so I was like, "Fuck it. I'm going to make it myself," and then I was back doing some theater. People always say, "You came out of nowhere." Well, I was around for a long time before I came out of nowhere.

HYLTON: How do you feel about working on small vs. large budget film projects?

LABUTE: I'm getting leery of working on bigger projects. You give up a lot of control on big projects, as there are other forces in play. Which is absolutely natural, because if it was me giving up that much money I would be looking over someone's shoulders too. But it doesn't make it pleasant. There are just too many people/producers involved, and they're all giving you notes and they all have some ideas as to what needs to be done to the film. I feel when you're hired as a director you're there to guide the ship. When I'm a writer and I have a director direct my show, I hand it over to them. When I hand it over to them I say what I think, but it's up to their interpretation of the work. I am able to compartmentalize it. I expect the same sort of a thing with film, but I probably shouldn't expect it.

A lot of these producers or studios want to make good films but even more they want to make money. It's a business and it's a business they've chosen rather than selling radios, but it is still a business. They would like it to be a good movie, but they want it to be a successful movie. Honestly, without the outlet of theater I probably would've gone nuts, both due to the time that it takes to get a film going and because of the way that they are made. You can see why actors, who give up more of their creativity, become directors and they write their own stuff and then become producers. They want to have some control over what they do.

But overall, you have to have an outlet. And I've been lucky because I've had places I could go and do my plays. I work hard on what I do and I fight for what I think is good. Theater gives you a much quicker turn-around time and immediate satisfaction, plus nothing ever beats the live experience.

HYLTON: So if you're a young writer going in to meet an agent for a first time how would you approach the situation?

LABUTE: It's hard to remember at times that the agents are working for you. It's a symbiotic relationship, but it's also parasitic. They are not bringing as much to the table as you do. They have certain gifts and crafts, but their ability lies in something else-- the arts of negotiation and introduction. It can feel like it's a job interview [when you first meet with them], but you should remember to have the confidence that they are wanting to have you on their roster. They should be selling themselves as much as you are selling yourself--you should be as sold on them as they are on you when you walk out of there. Don't be afraid of the notion that if it's not these guys, then it's going to be someone else. It can be very daunting, but remember, you wouldn't be through the door if they didn't think they could do something with you or get something from you. You have to go in with your head held high.

The good news and the bad news is that there is no one way to get in, no one path to success. Just find your door. It's different for everyone, but keep looking for doors because eventually you'll find one. You only need one opportunity. Keep beating the drum. Keep the

mental attitude of, "It's a matter of when, not if." Don't
let doubt even enter the equation.

EDWARD ALBEE

Edward Albee was born in 1928. After leaving Trinity College he moved to Greenwich Village and began one of the most lauded careers as a playwright over the last century. Albee has won a Tony Award for Lifetime Achievement, a National Medal of Arts Award, and Kennedy Center Honors. His play Who's Afraid of Virginia Woolf won the 1963 Tony Award for Best Play and was voted to win the Pulitzer Prize by the Pulitzer Prize Committee. However, Columbia University's Pulitzer Board found the content to be too controversial and rejected the recommendation, refusing to award the Pulitzer in 1963. He won the Pulitzer Prize for A Delicate Balance (1967), Seascape (1975), and Three Tall Women (1994). His plays continue to be produced regionally as well as on and Off-Broadway.

Chapter Eighteen

Afternoon, New York City

ALBEE: I moved into [Greenwich] Village in 1948. I
lived there for about ten years and then I wrote <u>The Zoo</u>
<u>Story</u>. It was a very important time in our culture because
there were many new movements happening. Most of
the abstract impressionist painters were living in the
Village. And you could go over to the Cedar Tavern and
watch them fall down every night. Or you could go down
to the San Remo where the poets and the writers were, or
the Carnegie Hall Tavern where the composers were. And
the most important thing is that everybody was doing
new work. Nobody was famous yet. Nobody had
agents. Nobody was suspicious of each other.
Everybody was cooperative. Everything was cheap. You
could get into everything and it was a very exciting time.
It was the last big explosion of new creativity in America.

You do not have amazing explosions all the time, you
know. Once every fifty years, maybe. So we had that and
it was very exciting. I learned a great deal about painting.
I learned a great deal about music. And I learned a great
deal about writing. And that was just a product of having
lived in the Village at that time.

HYLTON: Would you tell me a little bit about the writing you were doing at that time?

ALBEE: I was still writing some poetry back then. I was writing short stories and making a couple of half-assed attempts at writing a play... none of which I ever finished. The Zoo Story was the first play that I ever really completed. I was an adopted kid from a wealthy family and, fortunately, I got thrown out of their environment. And there I was, poor and living in New York City. Which was fine. I was doing odd jobs mostly.

HYLTON: What kind of jobs were you doing?

ALBEE: The job I had the longest was delivering telegrams for Western Union. That was a really good job because I could come and go as I wanted to, it was good exercise, and I got to meet a lot of interesting people. Some of [these people] turned up in The Zoo Story eventually.

HYLTON: And the plays you wrote in the meantime…

ALBEE: Well, I wouldn't say that I actually wrote these plays. I attempted and never got very far in any of them. At that time I was absorbing from everybody. Paperback books had just come about. I was reading everything. I was seeing all of the avant-garde European plays. And I was just absorbing as much stuff as I possibly could.

I think every writer has all of a sudden, if your talent is going to make it at all, a period when it breaks through. And it's different with every writer. For instance, Bernard Shaw didn't write a play till he was over forty, while Mozart was a better composer than anybody when he was six years old. People just have different periods of development. I think when I wrote The Zoo Story that was me coming into my own, or discovering whatever the extent of my talent is.

HYLTON: You found your voice.

ALBEE: Right.

HYLTON: What resources were available for playwrights at that time?

ALBEE: There were always some small theater groups around. I don't know when the Living Theater Group began. But it began sometime in the early fifties, I guess. The Poet's Theater was functioning in the early fifties. There were always a few theaters around that were doing interesting work. I remember I saw a play by Picasso in the early fifties in a theater in Greenwich Village. It was called, Desire Trapped By The Tail. And I saw plays by W.H. Auden and other people. And there were a couple of theater groups in addition to those. But that whole explosion took place around 1959 or 1960.

HYLTON: I understand after you wrote The Zoo Story you helped create a theater group in New York?

ALBEE: We changed the name every year. It was the "Theater Group of '62," then the "Theater Group of '63." After Who's Afraid of Virgina Woolf became a big hit, its two producers were making a bunch of money and taxes were very high. So we thought it would be silly to give the money to the government. So we started to establish this theater group where we would do the world premieres of new plays by American playwrights. We did that for eleven years. We did one hundred and ten world premieres by American playwrights. If you make money on the theater you should give it back to the theater.

HYLTON: So this came about soon after off Broadway ignited?

ALBEE: Yes, Off-Broadway was formed a little before that time. I think Off-Broadway existed by 1960 or 1961. I was fortunate though. With the success of The Zoo Story I didn't have any problems from there on doing my plays. But I think Off-Broadway and Kennedy's formation of the National Endowment for the Arts were very helpful to many playwrights who needed help getting work done in New York.

HYLTON: With regards to The Zoo Story, when you were writing did you do readings of the play?

ALBEE: No, people didn't do readings at that time. And I am opposed to most of the readings that happen in the theater anyway because they are not for the playwright's benefit. They are intended mostly to raise money or to do something terrible to the play to make it commercial and safe. In most cases that's what happens with a reading. No, but with The Zoo Story I finished the play and I knew a few people and I showed it to them. I showed it to some composer friends of mine who were some help. And it ended up going from New York to a composer, David Diamond, in Florence, Italy and then to Switzerland when it was translated and then to Berlin where it was produced.

So I was very fortunate in a way for an American playwright to have his first play done, not in America but, in a foreign country. I got a lot of mileage out of that sort of thing. That was nice. You know, "American playwright has to go to Berlin to see his play." <u>The New York Times</u>, bless it, wrote a nice piece like that.

HYLTON: How is it that you began directing plays?

ALBEE: I started directing a couple of stories after I wrote <u>The Zoo Story</u> because I was aware that the author of the play knows more precisely what he was after than anyone else does. So, if you can learn the craft of being a director, then you can save some time. So I started out being a really terrible director and then I became ok.

HYLTON: There seems to be quite a prejudice against writers directing their own work.

ALBEE: Well that's probably because most writers think conceptually and you can't direct conceptually. You have to direct specifically. You need to think not about what the character means, but what the character is doing. And most writers have difficulty or just plain can't make that transition. Beckett was a very good director. Pinter was a very good director. A number of us are very good directors and I think the reason for that is we can split ourselves. We can know what the author wanted and then get it from the point of view of a director. I imagine that a lot of directors don't want authors directing, simply because it takes jobs away from them.

HYLTON: Do you feel your work directing plays after writing <u>The Zoo Story</u> changed your writing?

ALBEE: Probably. I think I understood a little bit more about what worked and what didn't work. All of us get terribly fond of the sound of our own voices. And we all overwrite. But if you're a director you learn pretty quickly, "Come on, that's just self-indulgent. Cut that out."

HYLTON: I understand you spent some time with Thornton Wilder.

ALBEE: I was visiting a friend of mine at the McDowell Colony. And I had some poetry that I showed Wilder. And after reading [my poems] he suggested that I write plays. It was a nice indirect comment on my poetry. And so I started a few days later.

KEVIN HYLTON

Kevin Hylton was born in Washington, DC in 1974. He was an Artist in Residence at the 92nd Street Y for two years. He has had plays produced at Makor and the Tribecca Performing Arts Center. After writing for theater, Kevin began working as a screenwriter for Disney Animation. Kevin is currently writing and producing for film and developing several television series. Prior to writing for stage and screen, Kevin was a columnist for online and print magazines including <u>Playbill</u>, <u>Citizen Culture Magazine</u>, <u>and</u> <u>Viewaskew.com</u>.

Made in the USA
Middletown, DE
23 September 2021

48965252R00136